Finally! A book that puts body, mind a  rightful place.

—Clark V. Monahan, D.C., Director,
St. Augustine Physicians Associates

Dr. Dorian's book *Total Health and Restoration* offers the best and clearest understanding of body, mind and spirit and why so few chronic diseases ever get healed! If you only read one book on health and healing this year, read this!

—Charles W. Balaicuis, M.D.
Member, American Psychiatric Association
and The Florida Psychiatric Society

Total Health and Restoration is a book embracing God's perfect plan for man, which is to be healthy in body, mind and spirit. (See 1 Thessalonians 5:23.) Terry Dorian explains the healing power of food to maintain a healthy body and the healing power of faith to maintain a healthy mind and the connection of both. She has an extraordinary understanding of spiritual and medical healing, and I feel the reader will receive deep wisdom and insight for a completeness of life as yet not experienced.

—Teresa Allen, D.O.
Internal Medicine (UAB)
Diplomat of the American Board of Chelation Therapy
Fellow of the American College of Pain Management
and Schlerotherapy
Postgraduate Nutritional Pharmacology Training

I thank God for Dr. Dorian. Her new book opens the way to the abundant life! We need more writers who seek to minister health to a sick and dying generation! Congratulations!

—Norman L. Dykes, M.D., A.P.M.C.

Dr. Terry Dorian planned a nutrition program that saved my daughter's life! Now, Lady Holly, a New York Guild-certified Pilates instructor and a classical ballet teacher and choreographer, uses Dr. Dorian's teachings and books to guide her own clients and students. We are both eager to share Dr. Dorian's new book, *Total Health and Restoration,* with our dancers and everyone else who wants to be transformed—body, mind and spirit.

—LADY LEAH LAFARGUE
ARTISTIC DIRECTOR OF THE LAKE CHARLES CIVIC BALLET,
LAKE CHARLES, LOUISIANA, AND FOUNDER/DIRECTOR
OF THE LAFARGUE SCHOOL OF THE DANCE

A 180-DAY JOURNEY

TOTAL HEALTH

and

RESTORATION

SILOAM PRESS

TERRY DORIAN, PH.D.

TOTAL HEALTH AND RESTORATION by Terry Dorian, Ph.D.
Published by Siloam Press
A part of Strang Communications Company
600 Rinehart Road
Lake Mary, Florida 32746
www.siloampress.com

Unless otherwise noted, all Scripture quotations are from the Holy Bible, New Living Translation, copyright © 1996. Used by permission of Tyndale House Publishers, Inc., Wheaton, IL 60189. All rights reserved.

Scripture quotations marked KJV are from the King James Version of the Bible.

Scripture quotations marked NAS are from the New American Standard Bible. Copyright © 1960, 1962, 1963, 1968, 1971, 1972, 1973, 1975, 1977 by the Lockman Foundation. Used by permission. (www.Lockman.org)

Scripture quotations marked NKJV are from the New King James Version of the Bible. Copyright © 1979, 1980, 1982 by Thomas Nelson, Inc., publishers. Used by permission.

Cover photo, The Journey, by Wiley Hicks
Cover design by Judith McKittrick
Interior design by Pat Theriault

This book is not intended to provide medical advice or to take the place of medical advice and treatment from your personal physician. Readers are advised to consult their own doctors or other qualified health professionals regarding the treatment of their medical problems. Neither the publisher nor the author takes any responsibility for any possible consequences from any treatment, action or application of medicine, supplement, herb or preparation to any person reading or following the information in this book. Readers who are taking prescription medications should consult with their physicians before discontinuing prescribed medication and beginning a supplementation program. Do not begin any health or exercise regimen without the proper supervision of a physician.

Library of Congress Cataloging-in-Publication Data
Dorian, Terry.
  Total health and restoration/Terry Dorian.
    p. cm.
Includes bibliographical references.
  ISBN 0-88419-883-9
1. Health. 2. Nutrition. 3. Health--Religious
aspects--Christianity. I. Title.
RA776 .D684 2002
613--dc21
                                    2002012747

            02 03 04 05 06—87654321
          Printed in the United States of America

Dedication

To MY HUSBAND, R. GARY DORIAN, the iron mountain whose love, strength, protection and faithfulness to God rescue me from myself and undergird everything I do.

To our daughters, Kim (Mrs. Darren) Lancaster and Stacey (Mrs. Patrick) Dee (with greatest appreciation to Marge Osborne, their natural mother for her impact on their lives); and to our children, Jessica Dorian, Canaan Dorian, Christian Dorian and Jenna Dorian; and to our sons-in-law, Darren and Patrick, all of whose love, friendship and respect are our greatest treasures.

To our grandchildren, Preston Lancaster, Grant Lancaster, Brenna Dee, Haven Dee and Mazie Dee, whose lives are a constant reminder of the joy and blessedness of living in Christ, and to all of the grandchildren that God has planned for us from the foundation of the earth whose lives we look forward to in faith.

To my mother, Elouise Campbell Hicks, whose sweetness, self-sacrifice, compassion, giftedness, kindness, optimism and unconditional love are a daily source of faith and inspiration.

To my precious father, the late Wiley H. Hicks, my father-in-law, the late Richard Dorian, and my mother-in-law, the late Alice Dorian, whose dedication to their children and grandchildren continue to bless us all.

To Peter, Alfred and Connie Bunetta with love and affection.

To all our dear relatives in the Campbell, Childers, Hicks, Whitley, Parrish, Ellis, Blewitt and Dorian families with prayers for health and restoration.

Acknowledgments

I PRAISE GOD for making Dave Welday, Barbara Dycus and Carol Noe a part of my life. Their wisdom, encouragement, compassion, faith and the vision of Strang Communications made this project possible.

I PRAISE GOD for the love and support of Joyce and Bruce Marsteller.

I PRAISE GOD for innumerable ways that my church, Sunday school class and faithful friends bless our family and touch all that I do.

I PRAISE GOD for the intercession of Mike Fugate, Sherry Jackson, Eddie Owen, Ruth Chilen, Margaret Edwards, Viola Gibbs, Peggy Owen and Clyde Jones.

I PRAISE GOD for my sister, Debbie Hicks Ellis, and my brothers, Greg Hicks and Wiley Hicks, whose love and trust add worth to this and every endeavor.

I PRAISE GOD for the many practical helps and sweet attention of Jim and Jan Walsh, Sherry Hollingsworth and Sandy Hunter.

MY THANKS TO James Poe for the back cover portrait and to Ron Corn for the strength and flexibility training photographs.

CONTENTS

PART THREE
HOW WE HEAL

PART FOUR
A 180-DAY JOURNEY

THE FIRST MONTH

THE SECOND MONTH

Prologue:
The Journey

EXPERIENCING TOTAL HEALTH AND RESTORATION is a journey of the body, mind, emotions and spirit that encompasses the whole of life. No human being has ever lived who could show us how to make such an extraordinary journey—successfully.

No one can guide us moment by moment, number the hairs on our head and foresee the days of our lives. No one can tell us why we were born, why we suffer or why the world is filled with impenetrable darkness. No one can protect us from evil. No one can give us faith and hope when our world around us quakes with fear. No one can make us loving when we are the targets of blind hatred. No one can fill us with perfect peace in a house, room or relationship filled with strife. No human being has ever lived who can lead us every step of the way, wrap us in unconditional love and give us eternity—except one, the Lord Jesus Christ. Jesus is the Journey:

> In the beginning the Word already existed. He was with God, and he was God. He was in the beginning with God. He created everything there is. Nothing exists that he didn't make. Life itself was in him, and this life gives light to everyone. The light shines through the darkness, and the darkness can never extinguish it.
>
> **—JOHN 1:1–5**

Part One
My First Steps on the Pathway Toward Health and Healing

THE JOURNEY TO HEALTH AND RESTORATION BEGINS, for many of us, in the realm of the soul—an exploration of the mind, will and emotions. The first steps we take may not result in immediate dietary and lifestyle changes. We begin in small ways by contemplating change—just considering for the first time an altogether new and different lifestyle and imagining the health benefits that might follow.

All of us have the ability to become wonderfully stronger—physically, mentally, emotionally and spiritually—no matter where we are on the health continuum. All of us can achieve a new level of fitness at any point in our lives if we understand how we are connected: body, mind and spirit. With every hope, dream, laugh and open acknowledgment of our emotions, we build immunity and become more resistant to disease. Our culture has not always been aware of how our psyche influences our overall well-being.

A HISTORICAL WORLD-VIEW

Modern medical science, advancing so dramatically from the early twentieth century and into the twenty-first century, is rooted in the seventeenth-century world-view of Rene Descartes (the founder of modern philosophy). In Descartes' view, the mind and body are separate entities (mind-body dualism). Descartes had pragmatic reasons for creating this philosophical separation. The church of the seventeenth century regarded the mind as "holy," part of their exclusive domain and not subject to investigation by anyone outside the church.

Descartes struck a "deal" with the politically powerful church that resulted in ushering in the analytic method of reasoning. By taking the body out of the sphere of the "holy," he gained the freedom to investigate the body in the furtherance of medical science.

Historians regard the analytic method of reasoning as the greatest scientific contribution of Descartes. Analytic reasoning has proven useful in developing scientific theories. However, it was overemphasized in the twentieth century and has been wrongly applied to medical reasoning.

Today's conventional biomedicine is based exclusively upon analytic reasoning. Unfortunately, many complex ideas and entities cannot be examined solely by analytic reasoning. The body cannot be examined like part of a machine if we intend to understand, for example, the effect of stressful thinking on our bodies.

Modern molecular research has clearly established the body and mind as one. This fact has precipitated one of the great paradigm shifts that has exposed three centuries of flawed medical science. One acclaimed scientist, credited with establishing the biochemical link between the mind and body, explains the network connection in this way:

All of us have the ability to become wonderfully stronger.

> We know that the immune system, like the central nervous system, has memory and the capacity to learn. Thus, it could be said that intelligence is located not only in the brain but in cells that are distributed throughout the body, and that the traditional separation of mental processes, including emotions, from the body is no longer valid.[1]

Latest scientific breakthroughs prove that intelligence is not only located in the brain but extends throughout the body. Neuropeptides and their receptors communicate with the immune system. As we enter the twenty-first century, the significance of that research is having an enormous impact on science. In the last two decades of the twentieth century, psychoneuroimmunology (mind-body science) provided the research basis that established a fact most people already knew: Stress and anxiety make us sick.

When I took my first steps to health and restoration, the research connecting the mind and body was not yet completed. In order to understand my painful journey, as well as your own, it's important to keep in mind the flawed science (the old paradigm) that continues to regard the body and mind as separate entities.

The scientific breakthrough of molecular biology that connects mind and body only confirms the integration of body, mind and spirit as established in Scripture from Genesis to Revelation. Those discoveries, as we will explore later, began in the 1970s. During the following decades of the 1980s and 1990s, this new field of mind-body science—psychoneuroimmunology— overturned four centuries of flawed science regarding the connection between the mind and body. My journey to health began a few years before the beginning of those discoveries.

A Chance Encounter

In the spring of 1969, when I was twenty-two years old and newly married, my husband Frank and I had purchased a house in South Miami. Trying to acquaint myself with all the shops near the corner of Red Road and Sunset Drive, I wandered into a health food store. Since I had never actually been in a health food store before, I did not know what kind of store it was.

I saw a combination of food, appliances, books and row after row of vitamins. I knew it wasn't a pharmacy or a grocery store. Looking back, I can't imagine why I lingered, other than it piqued my curiosity. Had it been a typical sixties' counterculture health food store, I would have found it more interesting, but this place did not have that fascination. The shelves had an orderly, almost antiseptic look.

In those days, my hair hung below my waist, and I wore long, brightly colored, flowing dresses; I didn't even own a single pair of jeans. I didn't spend much time shopping for clothes, although I did spend a good deal of time in bookstores, stationary shops and any place with art supplies.

That day in the health food store I didn't have any interest in the rows of food, appliances and vitamins. It may have simply been the combination of books, food and appliances that caught my attention.

After browsing for a short while, I realized that the people who chose to sell those particular items had a plan, purpose and message. Once I realized that, I stayed long enough to listen to their message. I found the man and woman who operated the store to be very knowledgeable about health—a topic I had not turned over in my mind since my last day of health science class in fourth grade.

The couple seemed to be about the age of my parents, neatly groomed and conservatively dressed, but what I found compelling about them was their passion for health and healing.

I had never seen a wheat berry, an oat groat or organic brown rice before that day. I had never thought about grains at all, certainly not grains in that form, before they were milled into flour or flaked. I had no inkling about where in the world the grains all grew or who ate them. I examined the appliances, mainly a variety of vegetable juice extractors and water distillers. I asked questions about the foods labeled "organic," and I wanted to know why people consumed so many vitamins, minerals and what seemed to me an amazing number of different nutritional supplements.

> **We cannot accurately understand the human body by separating body, mind and spirit.**

Before I left the store that day, I noticed that this was more than a store; it was part of a movement. I also realized that what they discussed with me might actually be important—*absolutely foreign*—but important.

My Developing World-view

The sixties mean something different to each of us, depending on whom we knew, how old we were, where we lived and, most of all, what voices captured our attention. I think a lot of us who were in our teens and early twenties during the sixties regarded change as a good thing.

Many of us—young and old—believed we were part of something important. We saw problems, expected to find solutions and considered our personal choices and lifestyles as meaningful ways to impact our culture. Our lives mirrored the energy, idealism, contradictions, achievements and defeat of the decade.

When we encounter ideas that alter the course of our lives, it often takes decades to see and appreciate God's providence. The day I visited that health food store I had an unenlightened notion of health, as did a lot of people at that time, considering it to mean the "absence of disease."

"NORMAL" ILLNESS AND ADDICTION

During those days, I believed life was great most of the time, with the exception of those five days out of every month that I spent in bed, in a darkened room, comforted by a heating pad and a bottle of Darvon to alleviate the pain that accompanied my monthly premenstrual cycle.

That drug also typified the times. During the sixties, no one I knew ever used the term premenstrual syndrome (PMS). It wasn't until the 1990s that I learned about the two English physicians, Katharina Dalton, M.D. and Raymond Greene, M.D., who published in 1953 the first paper on the topic of PMS in medical literature. As a result of Dr. Dalton's enormous contribution to the understanding of PMS and her research on the astounding benefits of natural (bioidentical) progesterone, she is generally credited with coining the term *premenstrual syndrome (PMS)*. Her book *Once a Month,* regarded as the original premenstrual syndrome handbook, was published in Great Britain in 1978, followed by the U.S. edition in 1979.[2]

In high school, the adults I knew thought no more about letting their daughters take Darvon than they did about giving them aspirin. As to the health and safety of Darvon, later in the 1980s researchers began calling Darvon (near the top of the list of most prescribed drugs in America) "the deadliest prescription drug in the United States."[3] They attributed thousands of deaths and medical emergencies each year to its use.[4] Now, researchers tell us that there is only a slight difference between a therapeutic dose of Darvon and an overdose. That leaves a small margin of safety for any user. As though all of that weren't bad enough, Darvon's active ingredient, the chemical propoxyphene, is a relative of the synthetic narcotic methadone. Darvon produces psychological and physical addiction much as other narcotics do, often requiring the same treatment for those who become addicted.

Now, several decades later, I understand why staying in bed four or five days every month with a stack of good books was almost enjoyable. At the time, I would never have imagined that I had been taking narcotics every month since I was about fifteen years old. Later, during my years of research, I learned that conventional medicine has been, for decades, among the largest group of drug pushers in America.

Until I walked into the health food store that spring in 1969, the thought of seeking optimal health and longevity had never occurred to me. Like a lot of young people in their teens or twenties, I never thought about the connection between my dietary and lifestyle habits and my everyday strength and stamina. Before leaving the store that day, I made my way to a wall of books, booklets and pamphlets. After purchasing several armloads of reading material, I headed home.

> **The thought of seeking optimal health and longevity had never occurred to me.**

I also managed to overlook smoking as a serious threat to my health. As I write this, I shake my head. It's hard to understand how I could ever have thought or felt that way. My parents didn't smoke; my father detested smoking. Now I understand that when ideas and lifestyles hold us captive, the addiction begins in the mind, though we eventually become hooked physically and emotionally as well. When we change our minds about addictions, whatever those dependencies are, we begin the search to find strategies that will set us free.

EXPOSURE TO DIFFERENT WORLD-VIEWS

Despite the fact that I grew up in a Baptist church and was

president of the Baptist Youth Fellowship in junior high school, I had no inkling of a providential, personal, intimate God who is knowable and who wants to be known. Later in high school, I attended a summer speech institute on the campus of West Virginia University. I met a girl who had lived all over the world, and we became friends. She introduced me to Darwinian evolution and the author Ayn Rand. I read two of her books, *The Fountainhead* and *Atlas Shrugged,* that summer. Then I asked one or two adults about the Genesis account of creation and decided that my friend Robin was right. The Bible couldn't be the inspired Word of God. I still attended church, but I had lost the faith of my childhood, and I felt ridiculous for having believed the Bible stories and sermons for so very long.

After my sophomore year in college, I had no interest in organized religion. All of my ideas were consistent with a naturalistic world-view. All truth, I came to believe, had to be "scientific" truth, although I had no interest at the time in the natural sciences. Theater, English literature and philosophy held me captive. The theater of the absurd, Kierkegaard's existentialism and modern "confessional" poets (I discovered Anne Sexton before she won the Pulitzer Prize for "Live or Die") impacted and shaped my thoughts during high school and college.

Later I would learn that all of those shaping influences had absolutely no effect on God's providential plan for my life. His amazing grace and mercies enlarge the steps beneath our feet, until by His grace and mercy we are able to walk in the steps that He has chosen. (See Ephesians 2.)

THE DETERIORATING AMERICAN LIFESTYLE

There I was, a chain smoker since my freshman year in college, devoted to dark coffee with heavy cream and strong tea filled with cream and sugar. Like many people, I had spent a lifetime eating meat and dairy products. Having been raised by conscientious, educated and diligent parents, the meals in our home looked like photographs from the United States Department of Agriculture promoting the 1956 dietary guidelines: the Four Food Groups.

I considered my dietary and lifestyle habits as I drove home from the health food store that day. My carload of books prescribed many variations of a vegetarian diet. None of these discussions concerning healthy eating, contained in new library of diet and lifestyle advice, bore any resemblance to dietary guidelines produced by the United States Department of Agriculture.

The 1956 USDA dietary guidelines prompted my parents (and millions of others back in the days when most families regularly ate meals together) to say, "Eat your meat and drink your milk," at almost every meal. The USDA dietary guidelines in 1956 gave the meat and dairy interest, as well as the processed, devitalized bread and cereal interests, everything they could want:

- Group One—the milk group

- Group Two—the meat group

- Group Three—the fruit and vegetable group

- Group Four—the bread and cereal group

As I grew up, my parents, Wiley and Elouise Hicks, my two younger brothers, Wiley and Greg, my younger sister, Debbie, and I ate dinner together every night. Our evening mealtime was sacred. Dad had his own business, and if he needed to work late, he went back to the office after dinner. Everyone ate breakfast as well, and we didn't keep junk food in the house. Well-intentioned people trusted those USDA guidelines, just as they do now. However, since then world-renowned epidemiologists and enlightened physicians at our leading universities have denounced the 1956 USDA food guidelines,[5] just as they now condemn the 1992 USDA Food Guide Pyramid as poor nutritional advice.[6]

Sadly, at the turn of the twenty-first century the majority of men, women and children in America consume a steady diet of high-fat, high-sugar foodlike products that are processed, devitalized and chemically laden. These foods mimic the recommendations made by our 1956 USDA food guidelines. However, most people today consume far more junk food and strictly recreational foods than people consumed in the 1960s and 1970s. The sad reality in twenty-first-century America is that the dietary habits of most people are far worse than the guidelines recommended by the 1956 USDA Four Food Groups.

Dr. Neal Barnard, president of the Physicians Committee for

Responsible Medicine and member of the faculty of George Washington University School of Medicine, tells us the consequences of the poor health advice we as a nation offer the general population:

> The results are tragic. There are 4,000 heart attacks every single day in this country. The traditional four food groups and the eating patterns they prescribed have led to cancer and heart disease in epidemic numbers, and have killed more people than any other factor in America. More than automobile accidents, more than tobacco, more than all the wars of this century combined.[7]

In spite of the forceful recommendations by those in research and science, and their warnings regarding the connection between dietary and lifestyle habits and the rate of degenerative disease, American processed food, meat and dairy organizations won in getting USDA dietary guidelines that reflect their interests.

> On April 8, 1991, the Physicians Committee for Responsible Medicine unveiled a proposal to replace the Four Basic Food Groups. The Four Food Groups have been part of the U.S. government recommendations since 1956, but promote dietary habits which are largely responsible for the epidemics of heart disease, cancer, stroke, and other serious illnesses in this country. PCRM president Neal D. Barnard, M.D., was joined by Denis Burkitt, M.D., the pioneering physician who discovered the value of fiber in the diet, T. Colin Campbell, Ph.D., of Cornell University and the head of the ground-breaking China Health Study on nutritional factors in health, and Oliver Alabaster, M.D., director of the Institute for Disease Prevention of the George Washington University.[8]

Then, nearly a decade later in 2001, Walter C. Willett, M.D., chairman of the Department of Nutrition at the Harvard School of Public Health and a professor of medicine at the Harvard Medical School, wrote *Eat, Drink and Be Healthy,* the Harvard Medical School guide to healthy eating. Dr. Willett says this about the U.S. Department of Agriculture Food Pyramid:

Eat, Drink and Be Healthy tells you why the pyramid is wrong. Not merely wrong, but wildly wrong. And not just wildly wrong, but even dangerous...The intent of this book is to share with you what my colleagues and I have learned about the long-term effects of diet on health during the last two decades.[9]

MY NUTRITIONAL SEARCH

The information I found in many of those books I purchased in the spring of 1969 concerning optimal dietary habits would fore-shadow the landmark epidemiological studies published in the 1990s.

I couldn't wait to get home to tell my husband what I had learned. When I told Frank where I'd been, he sat down and listened to everything I said. I noticed that he had been beaming from the start of my monologue. When I finished talking, he told me about the health food stores he frequented in California and the spas he had visited in Europe. He was eager to hear what I thought about various dietary regimens.

When I saw that he was enthusiastic, I couldn't read the books fast enough. Frank was my confidant, my constant companion and very much my mentor. At that time, Frank directed *The Jackie Gleason Show,* produced live each Friday night from Miami Beach. He had spent a lifetime in television and was the first director of the first *Jackie Gleason Show, Cavalcade of Stars* (1952) on the DuMont Network (the first television network) where he worked as producer, director and conceiver of shows.

In 1969, the weekly tapings for the Gleason show ended for the season in February and didn't resume again until early fall. Frank and I were married in March of 1969, and we looked forward to the spring and summer to concentrate on whatever we wished. I quickly became immersed in the task of discovering the ideal dietary regimen.

At twenty-two, a week seemed like time enough to figure out the ideal dietary regimen. No mountains or chasms were visible to me, just life on an endless grassy plain. The mountains and chasms came later.

During my research week, Frank told me that he had quit

smoking several years earlier, and that if I chose to quit smoking he'd do everything he could to help me. I went back to my new friends at the health food store and asked them about nicotine. They gave me profound advice. If I fed my body nutritionally dense foods such as fresh vegetable juices, fresh raw vegetables and nuts and, at the same time, eliminated nicotine, caffeine and sugar, then I could overcome my addictions.

I spent the week devouring the books. The ones I liked best were those advocating "vegan" regimens: no animal products or by-products (e.g., eggs or dairy). The regimen I landed on as a place to start our health adventure featured vegetable juices (freshly extracted), distilled water (my friends did not sell reverse osmosis water purifiers), mounds and mounds of chopped raw vegetables (as many colors as possible), with fresh fruit and nuts for dessert.

It worked!

Frank said he'd follow whatever plan I thought best. That was, of course, quite a commitment. Frank, a Sicilian and an incredible cook, liked to entertain. In the year that we had known each other, I had tasted the most spectacular array of foods. He prepared amazing soups, vegetable dishes and a huge variety of meat and fish entrees. None of our guests would be nearly as excited about our new regimen.

Frank assured me there would be no problem. When we entertained, he would make his usual fare. I would prepare lovely salads. Fruit and nuts would be the optional dessert for those who did not want Italian pastries. Everyone would be able to eat the foods they preferred. That is exactly what we did, and it worked wonderfully.

We began organizing the kitchen. We kept a cabinet full of the herbs, spices and cooking supplies we needed for guests, as well as space for a number of special coffees and teas we served.

Then, I went back to the health food store to purchase a juice extractor, water distiller and produce for salads and vegetable juice. We bought organic produce when it was available.

For the last twenty years, all of the dietary regimens I have followed have been plant-based. I have experienced the therapeutic miracles of real foods. I learned the wonderful physical, mental and emotional effects of meeting all my nutritional requirements. Over the years, I've learned ways to optimize digestion and elimination and to build strength, stamina and optimal weight.

With the kitchen reorganization complete and the restocking, retooling process accomplished, Frank and I launched our new diet and lifestyle. Within a week of my first visit to the health food store, we had begun our regimen. I stopped smoking and eliminated all caffeine and sugar. I stayed on our completely raw food regimen for two years.

Our home opened onto three sides of our pool area, so the important element of exercise was met as we swam several times a day. With the new program, I definitely did not crave nicotine; I was too sick. For three weeks while withdrawing from nicotine, caffeine and sugar, I experienced nausea, headaches and vomiting. I had expected that; my unlicensed medical advisors from the health food store had prepared me for this detoxification process.

> **I have experienced the therapeutic miracles of real foods.**

The unpleasantness lasted about a month—a small price to pay for becoming a happy nonsmoker with no cravings and no addictions. By September of 1969 I no longer suffered from PMS. I had reclaimed those five days out of each month that I had lost from my adolescence. That is sixty days a year, which, for the last thirty-two years, adds up to five years and one hundred days of my life that have been rescued from a monthly disability.

A PAINFUL SECRET

Frank had his own goals. He wanted to lose weight and then maintain an optimal weight. What he did not tell me, and I did not discover until two years later, was that a decade earlier he had suffered two previous myocardial infarctions—heart attacks. Today, myocardial infarction is the most common cause of death in the U.S. About 800 thousand people annually sustain first heart attacks, with a mortality rate of 30 percent, and 450 thousand people sustain recurrent heart attacks, with a mortality rate of 50 percent.[10]

Frank and I met in the summer of 1968. Frank decided not to direct Jackie's summer replacement show. Instead, he organized a repertory company for the purpose of producing theater productions. I auditioned for the group in June of 1968. I remember thinking how great it would be to have a private conversation with him. As it turned out, we spent the whole summer talking, laughing, reading poetry and telling stories. I loved his stories and he loved my poetry. Even then we knew nothing could separate us.

The musicians went on strike in the fall of 1968, and the taping of *The Jackie Gleason Show* was canceled for a short while. Frank decided to fly to West Virginia and ask my parents for permission to marry me. I mailed a seventeen-page letter to my father prior to Frank's trip, and then flew to West Virginia to talk to my parents the day before Frank arrived. I knew Frank's age would make it hard for my dad and mother, but I was sure I could make them understand how I felt and why this marriage was right for me. I knew it would be difficult because Frank was thirty years older than me—and eight years older than my parents.

I was strong-willed and determined. I gave my father all the reasons why I knew the marriage would work, why Frank and I were close friends, why I loved him and why he made me so very happy. I also gave him all the reasons why I didn't think that men under forty were good candidates for marriage. He smiled, shook his head and gave me his complete support. Frank won their hearts, and we all agreed on a wedding at our house on Hilton Head Island in March of 1969.

Before I left to go back to Miami, Mother spoke to me very gently when we were alone in my bedroom.

"Terry, you'll still be a young woman when Frank is old," and then so gently, almost as a final plea, she said, "Frank could be dead in ten years."

I was brushing my hair when she started speaking. Her words sounded so hard, but Mother was never harsh or cold. She was then, as she is now, the kindest woman I have ever known. I knew she spoke with love. I answered her as softly as she had spoken to me. "Mother, I'd rather have ten years with Frank than a lifetime with anyone else."

In February 1972, after the Gleason tapings ended, Frank and I loaded up a crazy jeep he had rebuilt and headed for the mountains of North Carolina. We had purchased a vacation home and twenty-two acres outside of Asheville, in Leicester. A few days after we arrived, on February 14, Frank suffered a debilitating heart attack. Neither of us ever saw the house in South Miami again. We sold the furnished house while Frank was in the hospital. Friends in Asheville went to our house, packed up our personal items and moved them into our mountain home.

When Frank went into the intensive care unit, I found my way to the hospital chapel. I stood there for a few minutes. No one else was in the room. I couldn't pray. I had no faith. Now I understand that imagining we are alone in the universe, without the love of an intimate, personal God who knows us and loves us, is a deadly deception. But that day I left that chapel more alone, more shaken, than when I entered it.

I resolved to make Frank better by showing him how confident I was in his recovery. I remembered studying the James Lange theory of emotions in high school drama class. "If we put on the outer cloak of an emotion," we learned, "then we would begin to feel." That was the only thing I could latch onto at the time. Frank told me later that my confidence in his recovery did make him feel secure about the outcome of his attack; he believed he would get well.

Frank's physician allowed me to bring fresh vegetable juice and whatever else he wanted to eat to the hospital. At that time, there was a small health food store on Wall Street in Asheville. They juiced a wide range of vegetables for me each day, and I took the juice to Frank at the hospital. Our property was located twenty minutes out of town, so I appreciated getting fresh juice right in town. Frank consumed no hospital food. He gained strength and began to thrive.

It would be decades after those difficult times before I would come to a full understanding of the mind-body connection: that our world-views, our lack of a deep, sustaining faith and our unacknowledged emotions do impact our bodies at a molecular level. Psychoneuroimmunology, the science that probes that reality, had not been birthed yet,and there was no Dean Ornish program in 1972. Dr. Ornish's initial study (which took years to win broad support) was not conducted until 1977. His popular book, *Dr. Dean Ornish's Program for Reversing Heart Disease,* did not appear until 1990.[11] Now we have a wonderful protocol for reversing coronary artery disease—for those who know about it and are willing to change their lives in order to go on living.

> Today, through a course of clinical trials over the past twenty-three years (funded in part by the National Heart, Lung and Blood Institute of the National Institutes of Health), Dean Ornish, M.D. and collaborators have demonstrated that the progression of moderate to severe coronary artery disease often can be slowed, stopped or reversed by a program of comprehensive lifestyle changes, while diminishing utilization of pharmaceuticals. These lifestyle changes include: a low-fat, whole-foods, plant-based diet; regular practice of stress management techniques (including stretching, progressive relaxation, imagery, breathing techniques and meditation); moderate aerobic exercise; and participating in group support sessions...
>
> Studies show that patients have reported reductions in angina comparable to what can be achieved with bypass surgery or angioplasty without the costs or risks of surgery.[12]

Shortly after Frank left the hospital, we read Wilfred E. Shute's book *Vitamin E for Healthy and Ailing Hearts* (Jove Publications, 1983), proposing vitamin E therapy for the heart. We heard about the Shute Clinic in Canada and decided to fly to Canada so that Frank could have a consultation. They offered us protocols for vitamin E therapy, but nothing meaningful in the way of a therapeutic diet.

Home again, Frank walked our property daily. He struggled with emotions I had never seen him express. At times, he felt angry, frustrated and helpless. Then, one evening I found Frank sitting in bed. He was just staring ahead making very small chirping sounds. He didn't respond when I spoke. He was not "there." He couldn't hear me.

I telephoned Frank's doctor and described Frank's condition. The conversation was short. I remember it exactly:

"He's in a catatonic state" Frank's doctor said. I understood the word. I did not ask for clarification.

"What can I do?" I asked.

"Nothing. Just stay with him, watch him and let me know how he's doing."

"How long could he stay like this?" I was looking for case histories, stories of success that other people might have experienced with this sort of thing.

"I don't know," he answered softly.

"Will he come out of this?" I wanted some specificity here. What did he know from his professional training and experiences that would give me some help and hope?

"I don't know," he answered again, softly. What I remember most after three decades are those three words: *I don't know.* I thanked him and said I would call him later.

As I turned to go back to the bedroom with Frank, I suddenly knew exactly what to do. Remember what I said earlier, that while we are fumbling in the dark without God, He surrounds us with His light. This was one of those times, though I did not yet have a revelation of Christ, when the darkness simply got lighter and I began to find my way. I didn't know why my footing was suddenly sure. I didn't know that Jesus was there, enlarging the steps beneath my feet. (See Psalm 18:36; 2 Samuel 22:37.)

I gathered a few books and sat on the bed beside Frank. I read to him. Then I talked to him. I read and talked as though everything were perfectly normal. I talked about plans we'd made and how we could do this or that. I encouraged myself. Night became morning, and he remained the same, making those pitiful chirping, birdlike sounds. I napped beside him, but he just sat there. Then, sometime during that second day, he looked at me. He turned his head and looked at me. I knew he was in there hiding and that he would come out.

> **While we are fumbling in the dark without God, He surrounds us with his light.**

I don't remember any of the words I said that day. I just know that they were words of comfort, affirmation and my deepest expression of love. I told him who he was and where he had been. I told him why he would get well and how we would go on.

Sometime during the evening of that second day, he looked at me and began talking. He never realized his condition; we just went on with our lives. Months later I told him, after we had moved from Asheville and had a physician in Manhattan, just what we had walked through together.

PROBLEMS OF MY OWN

I developed a wide-range of stress-related disorders. I experienced terrifying chest pain and shortness of breath. After several episodes and several EKGs, Frank's doctor told me that nothing was wrong with me except that I was nervous and afraid. Although he didn't mean to be cruel, he was not helpful.

I didn't know that being nervous and afraid could make me physically sick. I felt humiliated and ashamed, very weak and very responsible for my own suffering. I accepted responsibility for being nervous and afraid, but try as I would, I did not have the emotional and spiritual resources to overcome all of my challenges.

One night, a migraine headache went out of control. I had excruciating pain throughout my entire body. Frank called our physician, and he met us in the emergency room. He prescribed morphine. I will never forget that injection. The euphoric sensation of the drug traveled from one end of my body to the other. In place of pain from head to toe, I felt not just pain relief, but also the most intensely pleasurable sensations I could imagine. When I found out the remedy to my migraine attack was morphine, I was horrified.

Then my physician prescribed Valium. Later that week I looked at the bottle and decided to take the medication. Two of the less common side effects of Valium are anxiety and a fast-pounding, or irregular, heartbeat. I experienced both and immediately called my physician, who of course told me to stop the medication. He wanted me to try something else, but I said no.

Once again, I sensed a dramatic clarity of thought: *I won't ever be able to solve this problem if I'm on drugs. I am making myself sick. Somehow I've got to find out how to get well.*

I won a partial victory over the migraines. I never had another episode like the one that sent me to the hospital. I tried to talk myself through what I learned years later were panic attacks. They subsided.

Then, just before we left Asheville, I began experiencing recurring episodes of anxiety accompanied by sweating, trembling and dizziness, which were relieved by small amounts of food. It became a constant concern. I never left the house without taking food with me. I knew nothing about hypoglycemia. I just thought I might be crazy. Fear became my shadow. Frank knew my symptoms and supported me in every way. I wanted to be strong and well. The only thing that felt worse than my fear was my feeling of shame.

Frank and I moved to Ridgewood, New Jersey, in 1973 to be near our physician in Manhattan. The day after we moved into an apartment near the center of that lovely village, I found my way to a health food store. The woman who owned the store offered me great advice and told me about orthomolecular medicine. She diagnosed my problem as hypoglycemia and recommended a physician in New York.

Frank and I made an appointment with the physician she recommended, Dr Harold Rosenberg, an osteopathic physician with a degree in nutrition. He told us about Linus Pauling's work and about orthomolecular medicine. I took a five-hour glucose tolerance test, and then began a series of treatments that turned my life around. Both Frank and I went on essentially the same regimen. We took megadoses of calcium and magnesium, a multiple mineral complex, a multiple vitamin complex and megadoses of niacin at home. In Dr. Rosenburg's office, we had B-complex injections, B-12 injections and calcium injections twice a week.

We began a dietary regimen that included small portions of fish, beef, chicken or lamb with every meal, large salads twice a day, one-half of a baked potato with every meal and a whole orange with breakfast. Frank felt great on that regimen, but it was much higher in fat than the Ornish heart protocol allows. This regimen changed my life and allowed me to manage the hypoglycemia.

Later, in the early 1980s, I learned to balance macronutrients (proteins, fats and carbohydrates) differently using intact grains, cold-water fish (high in omega-3 fatty acids) and an abundance of vegetables to keep my blood sugar stable. I dropped the baked potato and other high-glycemic carbohydrates from my diet.

It wasn't until the 1990s, when I discovered bioidentical progesterone, that I overcame hypoglycemia altogether. Then I was able to fast for a full day, exercise vigorously without concern about my blood sugar falling and live without the confinement of small frequent meals.

Dr. Rosenberg's megavitamin therapy ended my panic attacks. Frank bounced back to normal on the new regimen. However, as months went by, I developed a problem Dr. Rosenberg couldn't solve. I thought a great deal about my own mortality, I was nauseated most of the time, and I awoke each morning with dry heaves. I was not pregnant. Frank wanted to take me "home" to West Virginia, and for the first time since I had left for college at eighteen, no place in the world seemed more wonderful to me.

We moved to Parkersburg in the spring of 1974. I had lost ten pounds as a result of the vomiting. At 5' 9" tall, I weighed 115 pounds. Immediately I made an appointment with a family physician whose specialty is gastroenterology. He prescribed a little blue pill that ended the vomiting. It worked immediately. I asked him why I had developed the problem and why the medication had fixed it. The medication, he said, stopped the spasms in my stomach. When I asked why I got the spasms, he wisely answered that I needed to know what made me so upset. It took several weeks for me to get strong enough to stay up all day and begin a normal routine.

I didn't need a refill for the medication. The spasms went away. Frank and I bought a farm outside of town and a home overlooking the river.

During our regular visits to see my family we connected with one couple, Bill and Prudence Fields, who lived in Marietta, Ohio. We became good friends, and they too enjoyed theater and music. The four of us laughed a lot. Bill had met Prudence in New York after graduating from Harvard Law School. Prudence had grown up in Milwaukee, graduated from Northwestern University and appeared in *Funny Girl* with Barbra Streisand.

When Frank and I came to Parkersburg that spring of 1974, I learned from other friends that Prudence's life had taken, what seemed to them, a most amazing turn. She had become a "born-again" Christian and drove around with a Bible on the dashboard of her car.

Prudence and I had lunch several days a week all summer. She had decided not to talk about her faith with me until the Lord moved her to do so. She knew that I embraced radical feminism and Marxist socialism.

Then one Wednesday in September of 1974, she asked if I would like to go to church with her sometime. I was delighted to be invited because I could not imagine what sort of church group or gathering had persuaded Prudence to become a Christian. I had an intense curiosity about the people, the place and the message that compelled her to make such a dramatic change in her life. We had enjoyed our friendship all summer without ever addressing the world-view divide that was between us.

When Prudence asked me if I would like to attend her church sometime, I asked her when the next meeting would be, and she said they would meet that night. As an agnostic, fully convinced that modern science made it impossible to accept the Old and New Testaments as the Word of God, I wanted to understand how my very bright friend, Prudence, and her husband could possibly have become Christians.

> *I came as a spectator, not as a participant.*

I came as a spectator, not as a participant. The speaker was exuberant and filled with joy. He presented God's plan for redemption in Christ with love and tenderness, but I was not engaged in his message. They were words for other people who shared a very different world-view from my own.

Then, midway through the sermon, I was startled with a strange thought: *If this is true, I am wrong about absolutely everything.* A few seconds later, I found myself thinking, *I am wrong about absolutely everything.* Christ revealed Himself to me, just as He did to Saul of Tarsus (known later as apostle Paul) on the road to Damascus. It was as though I opened a door, and there I was, face to face with my Lord and Redeemer. In that instant, I exchanged a life of fear for a life of faith.

Frank made a profession of faith later that year, but peace and joy did not follow. His depression returned, and he continued to struggle with many issues that had troubled him since his heart attack in 1972. We moved to Louisiana in 1976. Once again, guilt and regret imprisoned him.

Then, in January of 1978, Frank came alive in Christ. He was able to articulate and accept his personal failure. Instead of punishing himself with Scripture, he saw the power of God's love and redemption. I believe he saw it then for the first time.

We had made it. The mountains had been so high and the chasms so deep. This awakening in Frank was not the unreality of the grassy plain. The Good Shepherd had led Frank into green pastures, beside still waters and renewed his strength. During those first three months of 1978, we praised God together in what became the most wonderful time of our lives.

FAITH TESTED

On March 30, 1978, Frank was sitting a few feet away from me, reading a chapter I had just written from my dissertation, when he had a massive heart attack and died.

We would have no more mountains and no more chasms. Frankie, as I affectionately called him, was safely home. That year I knew the divine comfort and sustaining power of the Holy Spirit. He gave me a revelation of Romans 8 that continues to define for me the reality of life in Christ:

> And even we Christians, although we have the Holy Spirit within us as a foretaste of future glory, also groan to be released from pain and suffering. We, too, wait anxiously for that day when God will give us our full rights as his children, including the new bodies he has promised us. Now that we are saved, we eagerly look forward to this freedom. For if you already have something, you don't need to hope for it. But if we look forward to something we don't have yet, we must wait patiently and confidently.
>
> **—ROMANS 8:23-24**

Out of my grief, I have learned to trust that God causes everything to work together for the good of those who love Him and who are called according to His purpose (Rom. 8:28). I know now that nothing can ever separate us from His wonderful love (Rom. 8:38–39).

No amount of pain or suffering is without meaning when we offer our experiences, our expectations, our hopes and our dreams to the Lord Jesus Christ in faith. By the power of the Holy Spirit, we are transformed by the difficulties and disasters we strive to avoid. Many of us find the path to total health and restoration when we are faced with challenges we cannot overcome mentally, emotionally, physically or spiritually in our own strength. Why? We recognize the reality that we are helpless without God, without a power infinitely higher than ourselves.

The irony is that when life is too comfortable we often become distracted by the material world and blind to the spiritual world. Yet, in pain, grief and hopelessness, we are able to see the futility of human effort and energy. By the grace of God, we are awakened by pain and loss to the ecstasy and abundance of living in Christ by the power of the Spirit.

I praise God for illuminating the paths of His choosing and turning our heads in the right direction. With this book, I trust that what I have learned throughout a journey of three decades will provide a way of escape for those imprisoned by affliction and affirm the vision of those seeking total health and restoration.

Part Two

America's Health and Healing Crisis

---

*The Least We Need to Know to Become
Part of the Solution*

KEY QUESTIONS

1. **WHAT IS THE NATURE OF THE CURRENT HEALTH CRISIS IN AMERICA?**

2. **HOW DOES THE CRISIS TOUCH EACH OF US PERSONALLY?**

3. **HOW DOES IT AFFECT THE HEALTH AND WELL-BEING OF OUR NATION?**

Chronic degenerative disease continues to increase at a catastrophic rate. Degenerative conditions such as heart disease, cancer, diabetes, liver disease, cerebrovascular disease, bronchitis, emphysema and asthma are among the ten leading causes of death in the United States.[1] Debilitating disorders plague a large number of people: allergies, autoimmune disease, ADHD, inflammatory diseases, pain, depression, eating disorders, insomnia, obesity, chronic constipation, migraine headaches, irritable bowel syndrome and many others. Each day, more and more Americans are in some measure disabled by these chronic conditions.

> *Chronic diseases are the cause of death for seven out of every ten Americans.*

FEELING ILL IS THE NEW "NORMAL"

In our country, feeling physically, mentally or emotionally ill for much or most of the time is considered the new "normal." One puzzling aspect of the current health crisis is the fact that, as the wealthiest nation in the world, we are also a world leader in obesity and degenerative disease.

A recent study, conducted on behalf of the Johns Hopkins University and the Robert Wood Johnson Foundation, shows that 125 million Americans suffer from at least one chronic condition, and 60 million live with multiple chronic conditions.[2] By 2020, according to the same study, half of the U.S. population will suffer from chronic conditions that consume 80 percent of healthcare spending:

> Chronic diseases are generally not prevented by vaccines or cured by medication, nor do they just disappear. To a large degree, the major chronic disease killers—heart disease, cancer, stroke, chronic obstructive pulmonary disease and diabetes—are an extension of what people do, or not do, as they go about the business of everyday living.[3]

According to the National Center for Chronic Disease

Prevention and Health Promotion, chronic diseases are the cause of death for seven out of every ten Americans. As a nation, 75 percent of the one trillion dollars we spend on healthcare each year in the United States goes toward treating chronic degenerative disease.[4] For the most part, it pays for the services of conventional biomedicine—physicians, drug therapy and hospitals. Conventional (allopathic) medicine is the dominant medical system, the authoritative voice for medicine in America.

Why We Have a Health and Healing Crisis

We pay the biomedical system for their services in treating the chronically ill, in spite of the fact that conventional biomedicine does not have an effective model for treating multifaceted chronic conditions. Andrew Weil, M.D. echoes the sentiments of many physicians, scientists and experts in the field of public health regarding the limitations of the biomedical model:

> You know, of the total number of sick people going to doctors, maybe 20 percent of them have conditions for which conventional allopathic medicine is appropriate. If we restricted that kind of medicine to that percent, we would not be in the kind of economic trouble we're in now. But we're trying to use this for everything and it doesn't work for the vast majority of problems.[5]

And according to other experts, cures are not forthcoming:

> We are left with approximately the same roster of common major diseases which confronted the country in 1950 and, although we have accumulated a formidable body of information about some of them in the intervening time, the accumulation is not yet sufficient to permit either the prevention or the outright cure of any of them.[6]
>
> **—LEWIS THOMAS, PRESIDENT**
> **MEMORIAL SLOAN-KETTERING CANCER CENTER**

> According to the Great Equation, medical care equals health. But the Great Equation is wrong. More available medical care does not equal better health. The best estimates are that the medical system (doctors, drugs and

hospitals) affects about 10 percent of the usual indices for measuring health.

—AARON WILDAVSKY, DEAN
GRADUATE SCHOOL OF PUBLIC POLICY,
UNIVERSITY OF CALIFORNIA AT BERKELEY

Wildavsky helps us understand the indices for measuring our health and shows how ineffective the biomedical system is in addressing the majority of those factors that influence our health:[7]

INDICES FOR MEASURING HEALTH

The biomedical system (doctors, drugs and hospitals) produces an effect on only about 10 percent of the usual indices for measuring health. Those indices they affect are:

- Whether we live at all (infant mortality)

- How well we live (days lost to sickness)

- How long we live (adult mortality)

This same biomedical system does not produce an effect on the other 90 percent of the indices for measuring health, which include:

- Individual dietary and lifestyle habits

  Positive characteristics: optimal diet, optimal exercise regimen, effective strategies in responding to stress

  Negative characteristics: poor diet, no physical exercise, smoker, poor response to stress, drug dependent (prescription, over-the-counter or illicit)

- Social, psychological and spiritual well-being

- Economic conditions: great wealth, dire poverty and everything in between

- Environmental conditions: home, school, work, community, state, nation and the world

- Genetic inheritance (e.g., genetic predisposition, biochemical individuality and an understanding of how to compensate for both)

Natural medical systems (sometimes referred to as alternative medicine) fully embrace the 90 percent of indices for measuring health that the biomedical system fails to address. The enormous range of nontoxic, noninvasive healing therapies—and most of all our mental, emotional and spiritual strength—gives each of us the potential for overcoming economic, environmental, genetic, diet and lifestyle issues associated with chronic debilitating diseases. However, the dominant biomedical system (known as conventional allopathic medicine), by failing to address all of these determinants of health, cannot cope with chronic degenerative disease.

The fact that preventable diseases kill seven out of ten Americans is a great tragedy for our country. That we spend 75 percent of the one trillion dollars allotted to healthcare each year on the treatment of chronic conditions is a grim reality. However, the truly horrifying aspect of this crisis is that those billions of dollars we spend treating chronic degenerative conditions go to conventional (biomedical, allopathic) medical doctors with no appreciable experience, training or expertise in effectively treating chronic degenerative disease!

QUALIFIED PHYSICIANS?

Conventional allopathic biomedical practitioners do not meet these basic qualifications for helping patients prevent and overcome chronic disease:

QUALIFICATIONS NEEDED TO EFFECTIVELY TREAT CHRONIC DISEASE

➤ A deep working knowledge of nontoxic, noninvasive medical systems (e.g., orthomolecular medicine, naturopathic medicine, functional medicine, homeopathic medicine, traditional Chinese medicine, chiropractic medicine and many other medical systems) effective in helping patients prevent and overcome chronic degenerative disorders

➤ A deep working knowledge of the relevant research

---

connecting dietary and lifestyle practices and the rate of disease

🖎 A simple understanding of the dietary and lifestyle habits of the populations in the world that do not suffer from our chronic degenerative diseases

🖎 Expertise, training and experience in providing optimal dietary and lifestyle protocols, as well as a wide range of nontoxic, noninvasive treatments and therapies that are effective in overcoming specific disorders (e.g., heart disease, cancer, Type 2 diabetes, lupus, irritable and inflammatory bowel disease, ADHD, allergies and the complete range of chronic conditions)

🖎 The desire to inform patients who have consumed the modern American diet for all or most of their lives of the benefits of an optimal diet and lifestyle

🖎 Motivation to be an excellent role model (walk the walk)

🖎 Intent to introduce the benefits of physical fitness to those who are not physically active by introducing (through multimedia presentations, interpersonal communications and personal demonstrations) the essential steps in rebuilding and revitalizing the body through exercise

🖎 Inspiring patients who have not developed the physical, mental, emotional and spiritual inclination to embrace change and who need a vision of health and healing

BIOMEDICAL ACHIEVEMENTS

Despite the fact that many physicians lack the qualifications for treating modern diseases, biomedicine continues to define and dominate "healthcare" into the twenty-first century. The lack of medical personnel who do not have experience in dealing with chronic diseases has left millions of people feeling frustrated and finding no relief or cure.

30

To balance that strong negative fairly, let me cite the positive. Most people in the Western industrialized world are reluctant to doubt the credibility of conventional medicine because biomedicine does wonderfully rescue us with the antibiotic treatment of bacterial infections, immunization, anesthesia and surgery, and it extends lives moment by moment.

To examine the crisis in biomedical healthcare is not to deny, denigrate or minimize the system that provides life support in times of crisis. When accidents, injuries or the acute stages of degenerative disease cause us to seek emergency aid for ourselves or our loved ones, we depend upon highly skilled physicians and technicians. We thank God for drugs and technological wonders that keep our bodies functioning when they fail to do so on their own. At those moments of crisis, when lifetimes of training for numbers of individuals converge and save a single life, we do not scorn the technology housed in multimillion-dollar hospitals.

We all know people who would not be alive today without medical intervention.

Many of us can never forget standing in the intensive care units across America, holding the hands of husbands, parents, children or friends who want to live. We do not condemn the excellence of biomedicine as a medical system with extraordinary expertise in preserving lives through drugs, surgery and technological intervention.

We all know people, many of us among them, who would not be alive today without medical intervention. Many others live and function extraordinarily well day by day as a result of hip replacements, knee replacements, organ transplants and other high-tech solutions.

Think about Mattie Stepanek, the profoundly gifted and loving eleven-year-old boy (and now best-selling author of three books of poetry) who is severely disabled and battling dysautonomic mitochondrial myopathy (a rare and incurable disease). His life, like the lives of so many others that have been blessed by the wonders of biomedical technology, gives us a glimpse of the very best that modern biomedicine has to offer. The breathtaking achievements of our technology can be measured by each moment of life that is preserved, expanded and extended.

Although Mattie's days are preserved and bounded by the medicines and ever-present oxygen that keep him alive, those machines and medicine do not define his life. Mattie's life touches us all, including those among us with disabilities, because at eleven years old, he has the wisdom and will to cherish the wonder of life and accept the circumstances with which he must live.

When we look at Mattie and others around the nation and around the world who cannot live without biomedical drugs and technology, we see the compassionate and wonderful face of bio-medicine. Without the scientific interventions of conventional treatment, we would not know Mattie. We would not have his poetry, which he says represents his "inner beauty." When we hear his poetry and thank God for his life, and the lives of so many others, we are ever mindful of the greatness in modern biomedicine.[8]

BIOMEDICAL LIMITATIONS

Yet millions of people are desperately unhappy about the outcome of treatments or lack of effective treatments for the wide range of degenerative conditions that plague our nation. We must acknowledge the limitations of biomedicine for the sake of millions who are not receiving appropriate treatment and the sake of millions who die each year from diseases that are *preventable*. While some people require drug interventions, surgical interventions or technical support to maintain a desirable quality of life, we have shown that even biomedical interventions cannot influence 90 percent of the critical factors on which optimal health and healing depend.

Many people look at the technological advances and breakthroughs in medical science and think: *A system that could do all that surely knows how to do the best that can be done for all the diseases that are plaguing America.* Sadly, the facts we have cited so far indicate that the biomedical approach to chronic disease is a death-causing system.

What we must do is look at the current crises in the health of individual men, women and children in America and examine the failure of those trained in "healthcare" to provide the expertise, information, training, goods and services that prevent and cure the chronic diseases that afflict us. In spite of the enormous achievements of biomedicine in the twentieth century, it is ineffectual in the face of chronic diseases, immune disorders and ominous new infectious diseases.

The billions we are spending on drugs and surgery to "manage" chronic diseases have proven to be a staggering waste of resources and human potential. For decades, natural medical systems with expertise in dealing with chronic disorders could have helped people overcome the disorders that are killing millions of Americans and disrupting the lives of millions more.

Yet biomedical physicians, with little or no expertise in helping patients prevent and overcome chronic conditions, continue to dominate medicine in America. Conventional physicians who accept payment for treating chronic conditions need to be trained to offer a great many more alternatives than drugs and surgery. If they do not have the educational background to treat chronic conditions properly, they need to find rigorous, multidisciplinary training from experts in those medical systems. Such training is available through a variety of means—distance learning, CDs, audiotapes and videotapes, as well as special workshops and conferences taught by experts in the field of Integrative Medicine.

Hopefully, early in this twenty-first century, health practitioners and hospitals who desire to treat patients with chronic diseases will need to demonstrate appropriate training and expertise in preventing and reversing chronic disease. They should become a part of the resolve at every level of our society to motivate, inspire and encourage great numbers of people in our country to adopt behaviors and lifestyles that help to prevent and reverse chronic conditions.

PROPER TRAINING NEEDED

All physicians and nonphysician health practitioners should have expertise and a commitment in the following areas before offering treatment to those suffering from chronic degenerative disease:

- Knowledge concerning what constitutes an optimal dietary regimen

- Knowledge concerning the connection between dietary habits and the rate of chronic degenerative disease

- Expertise in motivating patients to make dietary and lifestyle changes

- Knowledge of exercise management for persons with chronic diseases and disabilities

- A personal commitment to an optimal dietary regimen and a regular exercise regimen (aerobic exercise, flexibility training and weight training)

- Knowledge concerning stress-reduction strategies—the physical, mental, emotional disciplines—that prevent disease as well as heal, rejuvenate and restore the body

- Experience developing dietary and lifestyle protocols for patients suffering from a wide range of chronic disorders

- Willingness to teach patients essential self-care information and provide materials (e.g., audio, video and print) that will facilitate learning

- Willingness to offer patients instruction on the healing therapies that should become an integral part of daily life

- Expertise in medical systems that offer treatments and strategies for preventing and overcoming chronic conditions

NATURAL MEDICAL SYSTEMS OPPOSED

Many medical systems exist that offer expertise in overcoming chronic conditions. Among them are orthomolecular medicine, functional medicine, naturopathic medicine, traditional Chinese medicine, chiropractic medicine, homeopathic medicine, Ayurvedic medicine and others. Physicians and nonphysician providers who offer patients treatment for chronic disease need to be grounded thoroughly in the medical systems and healing therapies that enable patients to prevent and overcome chronic conditions. Many physicians trained in biomedicine have gained expertise in these medical systems as well. Members of the American College for the Advancement in Medicine (ACAM) list their areas of expertise and contact information on the doctor search area of the ACAM website: www.acam.org.

Naturopathic medicine, one of the outstanding natural medical systems, played a prominent role as part of conventional medical practice in the late nineteenth and early twentieth century—before industrialists established biomedicine as a monopoly. Then, as now, naturopathic physicians, like practitioners of other natural medical systems, conceive "the human body as a single, integrated organism—with effects on one part of the body having effects upon the rest of the body."[9] While early twentieth-century biomedicine eliminated that concept "from the mainstream of medical thought,"[10] natural medical systems are now validated by molecular research and clearly practice the new paradigm medicine that is consistent with cutting-edge research. Physicians practicing alternative medicine, functional medicine and naturopathic medicine have expertise in diagnosing and treating hidden food allergies.

These medical systems that provide expertise in treating and overcoming chronic disease have been opposed by mainstream healthcare and prevented from providing primary healthcare in America for nearly a century. The biomedical-pharmaceutical-industrial-governmental alliance, unhindered in monopolizing treatment, encourages the use of drugs and surgical procedures for the management of chronic diseases such as heart disease, cancer, noninsulin-dependent diabetes, asthma, irritable bowel disease, depression and a host of other chronic conditions. The drugs don't cure, but they do bring with them a wide range of side effects.

As a nation, we have spent a century finding and perfecting extraordinary, and often essential, biomedical solutions in the form of toxic drugs, surgeries and technical innovations to resolve a wide range of medical crises. The tragedy in all of this is that while we spent a century heralding the undeniable achievements of modern scientific biomedicine, we allowed the biomedical-pharmaceutical-industrial alliance to eliminate the essential medical systems we need in helping the people of our nation learn to prevent and overcome chronic degenerative diseases.

Conventional medical schools do not offer the essential training that physicians should have before treating patients suffering from chronic disease. However, biomedical doctors continue to manage chronic degenerative diseases using toxic drugs and invasive therapies, rather than using dietary and nutritional therapies, exercise protocols and a wide range of natural healing therapies. That is how the crisis has developed.

Every group in our country that has anything to do with providing healthcare services and educational training in health-related fields of study needs to be on the same page. Important groups include the legislative and executive branches of our government, public and private schools from kindergarten through graduate school, the National Center for Chronic Disease Prevention and Health Promotion, all schools of public health and the health departments in every community—to name only a few groups who need to work together in full cooperation.

PHYSICIANS WITH A MISSION

There are physicians who have recognized our staggering health crisis and have spent the last four decades reeducating themselves on their own time and at their own expense. They have studied treatments and therapies from traditional medical systems that offer many effective strategies for reversing multifaceted chronic conditions—strategies that are not provided by the biomedical community and are not covered by insurance. Those of us who have discovered these effective treatments, described in a variety of ways ("alternative," "complementary" and "integrative"), cannot imagine what the quality of our lives would be without having received appropriate treatment and therapies to overcome chronic conditions.

These astute physicians became committed to the mission of helping patients prevent and overcome chronic degenerative disease. They believe now, as they have for decades, that anyone charged with teaching, training and counseling individuals on matters of life and death must understand that *their primary duty to those whom they serve is to become a lifelong learner.*

Founded in 1973, the American College for Advancement in Medicine (ACAM) is a not-for-profit medical society dedicated to educating physicians and other healthcare professionals on the latest findings and emerging procedures in preventive/nutritional medicine. ACAM's goals are to improve skills, knowledge and diagnostic procedures as they relate to complementary and alternative medicine; to support research; and to develop awareness of alternative methods of medical treatment. (For a list of ACAM physicians and their areas of expertise, use the doctor search at www.acam.org.)

WHERE I FOUND HELP

Two natural medical systems that enabled me to overcome chronic conditions through nutritional supplementation and specific dietary protocols are *orthomolecular medicine* and *functional medicine*.

In the 1970s, when I discovered a physician in New York City who practiced orthomolecular medicine, it saved my life and gave me the understanding I needed to begin exploring megavitamin therapy. Many people with genetic predispositions or who have suffered from posttraumatic stress disorders benefit from megavitamin therapy and a variety of dietary and exercise therapies.

Then in the 1990s I began investigating *functional medicine* and later attended a concentrated program of study taught by Jeffrey S. Bland, Ph.D.: *The Nutritional Management of the Underlying Causes of Chronic Disease*. Along with these two effective medical systems, there is a third upon which I most often depend to find answers concerning the prevention and "cure" of degenerative disease—*naturopathic medicine*. These and many other natural medical systems are able, quite often, to "cure" degenerative disease, while modern biomedicine remains baffled by multifaceted degenerative disorders.

Soon after my search began, I realized that others had gone before me along this journey to health. I found this comment written by Julian Whitaker, M.D. regarding the influence of orthomolecular medicine on his life:

> In 1974, I met with four other doctors in the modest conference room of a Motel 6 to form the California Orthomolecular Medical Society. To my surprise and delight, one of my medical heroes, two-time Nobel Prize winner Linus Pauling, Ph.D., showed up to lend support to our fledgling organization. Dr. Pauling himself had

coined the term orthomolecular medicine in 1968, which he defined as "the preservation of good health and the treatment of disease by varying the concentrations in the human body of substances that are normally present in the body and are required for health." More than any other label—alternative, nutritional, natural, holistic or complementary medicine—orthomolecular medicine comes closest to describing what I have believed in and practiced for the last 25 years.[11]

A Crisis of Motivation

A significant number of people believe that we are in the middle of an unprecedented crisis in medicine. Few people believe that the biomedical-pharmaceutical-industrial-governmental-alliance will be able to reform itself because too many people have their time, energies and fortunes invested. This issue was addressed clearly at the Tenth Annual Convention of the American Association of Naturopathic Physicians:

> As the twentieth century "advanced"...the hegemony (dominance) of allopathic medicine came to be near-complete. First, it was the petrochemical and pharmaceutical mega-interests, and emerging professional class of medical experts, who redirected healing into a very narrow, reductionist, and self-serving approach...By the end of World War II, it was the government that started to become involved, again, predictably on the side of allopathic medicine. It was the era of centralized medical research—with power moving out of physicians' offices and clinics and into the growing bureaucracies in Washington, or to the allied academic facilities and drug company headquarters—all of them tied together by growing federal funding and regulation.[12]

Industry and Illness

Entire industries have been built on the new culture of illness. Patients feel alienated, devalued, dehumanized and betrayed by medical doctors committed to toxic treatments and drugs that produce side effects and only symptomatic relief.

Who then should accept the responsibility for the people who have died from degenerative diseases that are preventable? Who will answer for biomedicine's failure to provide appropriate treatment? Who compensates patients for the great losses in the quality of their lives? Patients and their families pay the price. Taxpayers pay the price. Still, this biomedical-pharmaceutical-industrial-governmental alliance continues to make billions of dollars in profit in treating chronic conditions.

Many patients with the time, education and financial resources seek alternative treatment inside, or outside, of this country. They often do find "cures" to the most obstinate and ghastly degenerative conditions. Others find help from books and newsletters, and they are able gradually to overcome degenerative conditions. All of us want to find physicians willing to acknowledge and embrace healing systems and therapies that work.

> *Entire industries have been built on the new culture of illness.*

Patients in need of healing for their bodies would rejoice if the search for wisdom in overcoming chronic disease somehow became as easy as going to their family doctor who is taking time to learn about nontoxic, noninvasive protocols for treating their chronic conditions. However, though the epidemiological studies have clearly established the dietary and lifestyle habits that prevent chronic degenerative diseases, most conventional medicinal practitioners do not focus on (or perhaps understand and/or personally practice) the essentials that would enable their patients to prevent chronic diseases—and to reverse them!

GOLIATH OF MODERN MEDICINE

The biomedical-pharmaceutical-industrial-governmental alliance that has dominated medicine since the early twentieth century, this Goliath of modern medicine, stands against all other natural medical systems that have expertise and experience outside the realm of biomedicine. With a war chest and the backing of the ruling powers, he swiftly secured a medical monopoly.

That monopoly, and the ethos that maintained it, continued to gain a stronghold during the first half of the twentieth century, denigrating other medical systems that had become dangerous competitors. This Goliath has created an ethos to mask his:

- Lust for power
- Determination to control medicine
- Unprecedented opportunity for financial gain

The forces behind the promotion of Goliath call the crusaders for other valid medical systems "unscientific quacks." They have even used that term to describe Linus Pauling, Ph.D., the only person ever to win two undivided Nobel Prizes and ranked by *New Science* magazine as one of the twenty greatest scientists to ever live, an honor shared by Albert Einstein and Isaac Newton. Dr. Pauling's scientific research, theories and ideas for the effective treatments for chronic disease, based on centuries-old traditional medical systems, were vindicated by research in the last half of the twentieth century and have recently been given honor.

Providing a variety of ineffective treatments for chronic, degenerative disease with drugs and unnecessary surgeries has created wealth and power for the biomedical-pharmaceutical-industrial-governmental alliance. The selfish motivation of this giant alliance has no regard for the millions of lives lost to chronic degenerative diseases that could have been prevented or overcome.

COMING TO POWER

What were our challenges at the turn of the twentieth century when this alliance came to power and so easily gained control over the practice of all forms of medicine? We were still reeling from the perilous devastation of infectious disease. Many people look back at the struggles of the late nineteenth and early twentieth centuries against the ravages of infectious disease and credit the development of modern scientific medicine with the eradication of those plagues.

Historians and economic analysts offer research that tells a different story. They attribute the major health gains made during these pivotal years to the expansion of the middle class. Prosperity gave people the ability to purchase soap, window glass and a variety of fresh and nutritious foods. Economists and public health experts conclude that the change of economic status led to greater hygiene (the blessing of soap) and consequent decrease in infant mortality.

Malnutrition decreased (the blessing of food). People achieved greater control over disease (the blessing of sanitation, better sewage, cleaner water and pest control). According to economists and public health experts, people enjoyed a longer life in the late nineteenth and early twentieth centuries as a result of these quality of life issues, rather than the efforts of modern medicine at that particular juncture. Infectious disease was on the decline before some of our wonder drugs were invented.[13]

In early twentieth-century America, a pluralistic medical system flourished, and conventional biomedicine was one of many healing systems. However, the practice of natural, nontoxic, noninvasive medicine did not have the political and financial backing to survive as an integral and essential part of our nation's healthcare system. Howard S. Berliner's authoritative account of the Flexner Report of 1910 gives us an insightful perspective of how that report established a new paradigm (i.e. scientific theory) of medicine:

> Conceptually, the image of the human body as a single, integrated organism—with effects on one part of the body having effects upon the rest of the body—was finally eliminated...
>
> The AMA's control over the licensing boards (i.e., the power to deny licensure to graduates of non-approved schools) proved to be the beginning of the end for the pluralistic system of medical care in the United States.[14]

From the beginning of the twentieth century and up to the present, most allopathic physicians, given the sole charge for tending to our nation's medical needs, have not limited their practice to those many areas of crisis care in which they have extraordinary expertise. Biomedicine has clearly failed to help patients prevent disease, maintain health and overcome chronic degenerative diseases. However, they *have* achieved overwhelming success in preventing a pluralistic medical system from thriving. As a result of these two undeniable realities, we have what amounts to a *healthcare holocaust*.

These champions of conventional medicine successfully established modern allopathic medicine (biomedicine) as the *only* legitimate medical system. They dismissed competing medical systems (such as homeopathy, naturopathy and virtually all nontoxic, natural healing systems) as inferior and scientifically irrelevant. Think of the death toll during all of these decades because conventional biomedicine failed to acknowledge its limitations.

Practitioners from other healing systems emphasize prevention and health maintenance first. Then, as chronic, multifaceted conditions arise, they use a wide range of nontoxic, noninvasive treatments that strengthen the body and facilitate healing. Many of the physicians practicing nonconventional forms of medicine, some of them M.D.s and Ph.D.s, struggle with current laws and regulations and endure the disciplinary practices of state medical boards in an effort to win back the freedom to practice medicine in America. This is a very sinister aspect of the health and healing crisis in our country.

Consequently, throughout most of the twentieth century, the majority of Americans had little exposure or access to the wide range of medical systems and natural healing therapies that offer effective strategies for preventing and overcoming chronic degenerative disease.

Many of us who did find our way across the country, and out of the country, to receive nontoxic, noninvasive therapies are alive and in optimal health today as a result. Americans at every level of society deserve the same opportunities. We found help in the 1970s, 1980s and 1990s because many physicians had begun reeducating themselves, as I mentioned, on their own time and at their own expense. Those of us who were able to find effective medical help described as "alternative," "complementary" and "integrative" are grateful.

DEALING WITH A MEDICAL MONOPOLY

Our government, in alliance with biomedical, pharmaceutical and insurance interests, still supports the biomedical monopoly on healthcare. At a time in our history when chronic degenerative disease has become an epidemic, we need a wide range of medical systems that are effective in helping people prevent and overcome chronic conditions. Medical systems with great expertise in treating complex, multifaceted disorders need to become mainstream, sharing the funding, credibility and authority of biomedicine.

Patients go to physicians with the hope that they will receive the best help available. They pay (or their insurance pays) for what the patient hopes will be effective treatment. Effective nontoxic, noninvasive treatment for heart disease and cancer should be widely available. Biomedical physicians should be required to make a full disclosure of the dangers connected with various conventional biomedical practices. A leading consumer group in California, California Citizens for Health Freedom, through legislative advocacy efforts, is seeking laws that guarantee such disclosures, demanding that physicians reveal safe alternatives to toxic treatments and services:

FULL DISCLOSURE REQUESTS

- Discuss alternatives to the use of mercury in dental fillings.

- Discuss alternatives to the use of psychotropic drugs, such as Ritalin, in treating a wide range of disorders.

- Discuss effective orthomolecular treatments for the mentally ill as opposed to the standard practice of prescribing the long-term use of prescription drugs.

- Discuss alternatives to chemotherapy, radiation and surgery in treating each type of cancer, providing statistics for the success of alternative treatments and the standard protocols recommended by oncologists.

- Discipline gynecologists who fail to warn women of the dangers of hysterectomies and who fail to provide meaningful information concerning the alternatives to hysterectomies.

- Discuss nutritional intervention programs with the parents of children with Down's syndrome and provide the research indicating that nutritional therapy can increase intelligence.

> ◦ Discuss the dangers of certain drugs given during childbirth that may cause autism in children, and discuss the possible side effects of all drugs given during childbirth.

The fact that biomedical physicians in great number are resistant to any and all alternatives to drugs and surgery indicates the pressing need to end the monopoly and allow patients to choose primary care providers who can best meet their needs.

THE NEED TO END THE MEDICAL MONOPOLY

Orthomolecular medicine and functional medicine represent the best research in science and medicine during the last half of the twentieth century. Homeopathic medicine and naturopathic medicine originated as early as the nineteenth century. Traditional Chinese medicine and Ayurvedic medicine combine centuries of effective treatments with current research documenting the effectiveness of nontoxic, noninvasive treatments for chronic degenerative disease.

Misdiagnosis is yet another crisis in healthcare.

All of these proven medical systems offer expertise in disease prevention and self-care, and they develop strategies for helping patients make difficult dietary and lifestyle changes.

On December 15, 1995, the Cato Institute published a Policy Analysis titled "The Medical Monopoly: Protecting Consumers or Limiting Competition?" The report concludes that consumers are not being protected and that they have the right to choose effective and appropriate healthcare. However, those rights are being denied; it is time for us to end the medical monopoly.[16]

Peter Chowka gives us additional insight into the realities we face as a nation of chronically ill people:

> Orthodox medicine is useful in dealing with things like emergencies and trauma, and in performing high tech surgeries. But in terms of the increasing incidence and death rates from cancer, AIDS, diabetes, and

44

Alzheimers and the persistence of heart disease, stroke, and hypertension as the leading causes of death and disability...our society's organized efforts against and standard ways of treating most chronic diseases have become Medical Vietnams...

The premise, like in Vietnam, is that you can search out and destroy disease, using toxic, even deadly weapons. This philosophy denies how the body actually works and how it truly can be healed, or how it can be encouraged to heal itself.[17]

THE TRAGEDY OF DEATH BY PHYSICIANS

Peter Chowka also mentioned the increase in iatrogenic disease (medical mistakes).[16] He spoke as an insider and journalist with the wisdom and instincts to "know" the story. Subsequent reports published in major medical journals have confirmed this tragedy of doctor-related deaths.

Misdiagnosis is yet another crisis in healthcare, costing the lives of millions, as a result of a biomedical monopoly uncensored by the rigorous competition of market forces. By closing out all of the competition, the monopoly eliminates the very platform from which physician and nonphysician health practitioners from other medical systems can warn consumers about the abuses within any system of medicine.

In 1999, the Committee on Quality healthcare at the Institute of Medicine published their report of death by iatrogenic causes in a book called *To Err Is Human: Building a Safer Health System*.[18] Their report revealed that:

- In any given year 98,000 people die from medical errors that occur in hospitals.

- More people die from iatrogenic deaths than die from motor vehicle accidents, breast cancer or AIDS—each of which receive far more public attention.

- More people die tragically from medication errors alone than suffer injuries in workplaces throughout America.

To Err Is Human did indeed break the silence surrounding the horrific consequences of medical mistakes. In a fair manner, they

45

don't condemn individual health professionals for making honest mistakes, but rather set forth a national agenda—with state and local implications—for reducing medical errors and providing patients with a health system that meets minimal standards for safety.

Following that report, Barbara Starfield, M.D., of the Department of Health Policy and Management, Johns Hopkins School of Hygiene and Public Health, wrote a landmark article published in *JAMA (Journal of the American Medical Association)*, in which she revealed that medical mistakes are the third leading cause of death in the United States. Each year approximately 225,000 people die of iatrogenic causes.[19] The breakdown of annual deaths caused by the combination of medical mistakes and the adverse effects of medication is as follows:

Medical mistakes are the third leading cause of death of Americans.

- 12,000—unnecessary surgeries

- 7,000—medication errors in hospitals

- 20,000—other errors in hospitals

- 80,000—infections in hospitals

- 106,000—non-error, negative effects of drugs[20]

HOW SHOULD WE THEN RESPOND?

When the United States dropped the atomic bomb on Hiroshima and Nagasaki on August 6, 1945, the atomic blasts killed 185,000 people. The terror of so many people killed at one time gripped Japan and the rest of the world. That tragedy impacted the end of hostilities on August 15, 1945 when the Imperial Japanese Government agreed to unconditional surrender.

Without minimizing that horrible event, how can we account for the fact that 225,000 people dying each year from medical mistakes escape our attention? Why doesn't the media stay on this story? Is it that we do not recognize this as a holocaust? Is it because we believe that conventional allopathic medicine is as good as it gets?

Why—in the face of millions of people dying from preventable disease, or dying because they did not receive effective treatment for a wide range of chronic conditions or from iatrogenic causes—have responsible American citizens not stormed our nation's capital and demanded an end to the terror? The numbers of dead are staggering. The battle is real, and this is a war we can win.

Conventional allopathic medicine as institutionalized by the biomedical-pharmaceutical-industrial-governmental alliance has created a Marxist medical system in which industry, in cooperation with biomedicine and government, controls the means of production. This is not straightforward capitalism as we know it.

Through licensure, this powerful alliance prevents all other medical systems from producing and distributing goods (appropriate treatments and a wide range of nontoxic, noninvasive therapies) and blocks consumer access to the services of physician and nonphysician healthcare providers. This biomedical monopoly determines what treatments are appropriate for the full range of degenerative diseases, imposes biomedical protocols, drugs and surgeries as they deem appropriate and denies other medical systems the right to provide the effective treatments that consumers want and need.

And this alliance, by imposing a medical monopoly on America, continues to enmesh honorable, dedicated and talented biomedical physicians in a degrading web of corruption, power and privilege. As consumers rise up and demand access to all available medical systems and healing therapies, conventional biomedical practitioners need to respond as well, standing beside us—or they too will be tainted by the system that is responsible for the death of millions of people.[21]

RESPONSE OF THE MEDICAL COMMUNITY

Throughout the 1990s, major newspapers across the country began reporting the prevalence of iatrogenic deaths. Physicians across the country knew. Here is a sample of the desire to keep reports of iatrogenic death from reaching the news media:

> In what may be an unprecedented step, the University of Kentucky Chandler Medical Center is requiring its faculty physicians to sign an agreement promising not to make "disparaging remarks" about doctors in private

practice across the state, or their patients. UK residents—doctors in training—are required to sign a similar pledge. Dr. Emery Wilson, the dean of the UK medical school and the author of the new policy, insists it is no gag order.[22]

How did the American Medical Association view this publicity that iatrogenic deaths were receiving? Thinking about this topic, I wondered how executives representing the major advocacy group for biomedical physicians, the AMA, might be talking to themselves and to other members in the late 1990s. How did they view conventional medical practice during the last decade of the twentieth century? What plans were they going to make in response to their catastrophic failure in helping individual Americans to prevent degenerative disease and to overcome chronic disorders?

In December of 1998, the American Medical Association's House of Delegates conducted an Interim Meeting in Honolulu, Hawaii. Dr. E. Ratcliffe Anderson, Jr., executive vice president, included the following remarks in his address:

> We are the AMA. And no other organization does what we do. Not just promoting the art and science of medicine, and the betterment of the public health—work that we have done for a century and a half and more. But standing tall as the stewards of medicine. The champions of ethics. And the voice of advocacy and the highest medical standards. Valuable work. Essential work...
>
> More than anything, we are the stewards of medicine's time-honored standards. We are the guardians of our present progress. We are the beacon of the future. And those who hold the vision of medicine as it can and must be now, and for the 21st century.[23]

As I read his speech, I kept hearing Jackie Gleason's character, Ralph, from the television show *The Honeymooners:* "I'm the king, Alice! I'm the king!"

However, this speaker was serious—dead serious—sounding very much like the lord chancellor of some mythical medical kingdom.

From the very beginning of our republic, people foresaw the danger of having any one medical system control access to all the others. Benjamin Rush, M.D., George Washington's personal physician and a signer of the Declaration of Independence, warned his countrymen of the dangers of government control of medicine:

> Unless we put medical freedom into the Constitution, the time will come when medicine will organize into an undercover dictatorship...To restrict the art of healing to one class of men and deny equal privileges to others will constitute the Bastille of medical science. All such laws are un-American and despotic and have no place in a republic...The Constitution of this republic should make special privilege for medical freedom as well as religious freedom.[24]

We will find our voice as a nation. We must. Millions of lives continue to be lost because free access to medical systems with qualified physician and nonphysician health practitioners has been denied to Americans. Chronic disease is bankrupting our nation, and we are losing our friends and loved ones to diseases that they could have prevented and quite possibly overcome.

Integrative physicians trained in biomedicine, researchers at our leading institutions, physician and nonphysician health practitioners from across many medical systems and consumer groups across the nation are working to end the medical monopoly and make it possible for a robust pluralistic medical system to flourish and to meet the needs of our nation.

Sometime during the twentieth century going to the "doctor" began to mean going to a conventional, allopathic physician trained in biomedicine. A great number of Americans do not know what types of natural healing systems are available. However, consumers are driving the move for greater access to the treatments and therapies they want and need. This move for safe and effective healthcare will not end.

SUMMARY: KEY ISSUES IN AMERICA'S HEALTH AND HEALING CRISIS

Spending 75 percent of one trillion dollars each year on a medical system that lacks expertise in chronic degenerative disease is intolerable. The numbers and varieties of chronic disease are growing at a catastrophic rate, with heart disease the number one cause of death in men and women.

According to the American Heart Association, heart disease and stroke will cost the U.S. almost $330 billion in 2002. Of this $330 billion, $199 billion will be spent for direct medical costs. Loss of productivity during illness ($31 billion) and loss of future productivity due to premature death ($99 billion) are the other major costs.[25]

While modern biomedicine has made its greatest strides in the area of acute care, conventional healthcare providers are among the least prepared to help patients prevent and overcome the debilitating effects of these chronic degenerative conditions. To clarify the present role of allopathic medicine, we need to understand the following facts:

- *Allopathy* is a term generally used to describe Western medicine, whereby the treatment of disease is approached by the use of remedies (such as drugs or surgery) that create the opposite effect to those produced by the disease.[26]

- Official medicine (i.e., biomedicine) has more sources of political and financial power than does traditional medicine (i.e. ethnomedicine); the latter has had to struggle for legitimacy against influential forces.

- Biomedical technology often determines what is considered authoritative knowledge and, in turn, establishes a particular domain of power. Biomedicine typically extends this privileged position to economics, politics and class relationships; its power is jealously guarded by legislation, medical schools, licensing regulations and medical terminology.[27]

- Most consumers who suffer from chronic disease seek help from conventional, allopathic healthcare providers because biomedicine is the only fully approved system. Insurance coverage is critical for most people, and conventional allopathic medicine is the system sanctioned by the public-private healthcare financing system.

🐀 The pharmaceutical industry markets and supports bio-medicine; in return, biomedicine promotes its drugs. The *Journal of the American Medical Association* has documented the inappropriate interactions between physicians and companies manufacturing drugs.[28] The pharmaceutical industry supports biomedical physicians and influences their medical education. An article in *Lancet* documents the relationship between medical education activities, the pharmaceutical industry, and medical education services suppliers (MESS).[29]

🐀 During the first half of the twentieth century, a biomedical-pharmaceutical-industrial-governmental alliance successfully established allopathic medicine as the dominant medical system, giving conventional biomedicine the credibility, authority and power to limit, and in most cases eliminate, competition from other medical systems.

🐀 Advances in the natural sciences—quantum theory, relativity theory and molecular theory—give us the "hard science" that expose the flaws and limitations of seventeenth-century science, as well as the false assumptions on which the modern scientific biomedical model is based.

Consumers in search of optimal treatments for chronic conditions suffer while the old paradigm of the medical establishment reigns and rules, refusing to admit its limitations. This powerful biomedical regime guards its power to secure its dominance over other medical systems by controlling billions of dollars in funding to further research. And it continues to oppose the advancement of physicians and scientists who operate within a new paradigm based on other valid medical systems.

AN INEVITABLE PARADIGM SHIFT

Thomas Kuhn, American historian of science, is often credited with coining the term *paradigm shift,* which means "the radical change in perspective of moving someone from one sphere of scientific theories or ideas into another sphere." However, many scholars think that it is more accurate to say that Kuhn popularized the term with his book *The Structure of Scientific Revolutions,* which is widely regarded as one of the most influential works of history and philosophy of the twentieth century.[30]

Paradigms, according to Thomas Kuhn, must meet two requirements:

- First, they must be truly unprecedented in such a way that they actually compel those who are involved in the competing scientific model to reassess that model and to commit fully to the new scientific theory. They must leave the old world of ideas and activities and embrace the new.

- Second, the new world of ideas must be uniquely expandable, leaving a wide range of problems for those devoted to the new scientific theory to solve.

Kuhn's work enables us to recognize the enormity of this decision to leap into another world of ideas and activities; it is that sort of leap that is a true paradigm shift according to Kuhn. Such a shift can create a crisis evoking fear and excitement. Albert Einstein wrote of his crisis: "It was as if the ground had been pulled out from under one, with no firm foundation to be seen anywhere, upon which one could have built."[31]

> **A great scientific system for relieving pain and suffering can also become a sinister force.**

What does it take to initiate interest in a radically new direction and to galvanize support for positions contrary to the scientific establishment? Kuhn suggests that young scientists or scientists new to the field are often the ones who instigate paradigm shifts. Unmolested by entrenched allegiances to any particular set of rules or a paradigm, these are the ones who are generally successful in challenging existing world-views.[32]

Thomas Kuhn's essay also helps us understand how a great scientific system for relieving pain and suffering can also become a sinister force, so very blind to its own limitations that it rejects a wholly effective, but different group of scientific activities and solutions. Modern medical science is a great force for relieving pain and suffering; it is also a sinister force because it will not recognize its own limitations, nor will it honor the strength and solutions of the other medical systems.

OLD PARADIGM VS. NEW PARADIGM

It is vital to understand that Thomas Kuhn did not disparage old paradigms. He learned to value the old and the new as different ways of looking at the same thing. We need both the old and new to address our health crisis.

To create a paradigm shift in the modern medical monopoly, armies of vocal and voting Americans must organize and demonstrate their support for the new paradigm scientists and M.D.s. Perhaps the first item of business will be to persuade Congress to pass measures allotting half of the real estate at the National Institutes of Health to the medical systems that are currently barred from mainstream medicine.

Within this new paradigm, scientists and medical doctors can then receive full funding and support as they study, document solutions and continue to develop protocols for the prevention and cure of degenerative disease. The arrangement now is quite different. The National Center for Complementary and Alternative Medicine (NCCAM), although under its own immediate director, is still very much monitored by old paradigm scientists and medical doctors.

In the new arrangement, the only thing that the old paradigm and new paradigm scientists would share would be free access to the hundreds of lawn-covered acres at the National Institutes of Health. As to the sixty-five all brick buildings housing the laboratories and offices of the National Institutes of Health in a suburb of Washington, D.C., they would be divided equally between the two groups. Of course, the annual congressional appropriations for the National Institutes of Health would be divided between the two paradigms. Under this splendid arrangement, there would be no arguments—just everyone doing what he or she knows how to do best for the benefit of all Americans.

Two different directors at the National Institutes of Health, each working in separate sections of the buildings, each managing entirely different groups of people and facilitating different spheres of scientific theories and ideas, would be an important step in resolving America's health and healing crisis. This arrangement would go a long way in correcting the gross inequity that now exists.

The entire $23 billion annual funding at National Institutes of Health currently supports the old paradigm. No other world-view has control over the funding. This, despite the fact that none of the activities at the National Institutes of Health have helped to prevent the catastrophic rise in multifaceted chronic degenerative conditions or provided nontoxic, noninvasive healing therapies for overcoming them.

We need Congress, after hearing a clear and unified message from voting Americans, to enact legislation ending the medical monopoly. Only then will this modern-day Goliath, the biomedical-pharmaceutical-industrial-governmental alliance, come to an end. Then we can begin to recover from the healthcare holocaust and work to educate the nation in ways to prevent and reverse chronic conditions.

LEARNING TO ASK THE RIGHT QUESTIONS

When we think about the current healthcare crisis, we need to ask reasonable questions, such as: *How can we look to this same medical system—biomedicine—for solutions when they have presided over decades of failure?*

As we have discussed, the National Institutes of Health (NIH), as the world's foremost medical research institution, is where our government looks for answers to the nation's most pressing health questions. It receives billions of dollars of funding for research to find those answers.

While we spend 75 percent of one trillion dollars in treating chronic degenerative disease, the president's budget request for the National Center for Complementary and Alternative Medicine (NCCAM) for fiscal year 2002 is a mere $100,063,000.[33] *An important question this center should be asking is: What eminent group of scientists outside your paradigm is going to critically review the quality of your evaluation of medical treatments and healing systems that are well beyond the paradigm within which you currently operate?*

Our government currently supports all efforts by conventional allopathic medicine to block consumer access to a full range of effective healing systems. Thousands of patients have spent years fighting for the right to receive the medical treatment that they want and need. Consumers are fighting all across America for the right to receive noninvasive, nontoxic therapies for debilitating, life-threatening chronic conditions.

In 1997, Americans paid 629 million visits to alternative medical providers. They made 326 million visits to biomedical physicians in the same year. In an attempt to prevent or treat their disorders, more than 80 million Americans are spending $32 billion in visits to alternative practitioners. They paid more than half of that amount out-of-pocket.[34]

Perhaps the NCCAM should interview the patients who choose alternative medical practitioners and learn about the effects that nontoxic, noninvasive therapies have on these patients. They should ask these patients why they spend years of their lives fighting for the right to access appropriate treatment.

Perhaps researchers from NCCAM should also interview the thousands of patients around the country who have overcome chronic debilitating conditions to find out what their integrative physicians have done that works. In return, the patients they interview would probably ask why the current laws, regulations and discipline practices of the state medical boards still prevent them from accessing nontoxic, noninvasive and, most of all, effective therapies. This question is especially appropriate in view of the fact that the NCCAM exists and has over $100 million budgeted to them.

Within the academic community, and certainly in the general population, there is much support for free access to all medical systems. The following chart shows the strong support there is presently for CAM (Complementary and Alternative Medicine) therapies:[35]

INTEREST IN CAM THERAPISTS

- 80 percent of medical students want training in CAM.

- 70 percent of family physicians want training in CAM.

- 69 percent of Americans use unconventional medical therapies.

OMINOUS NEWS FROM THE INSIDE

Many of the world's best research scientists work at the National Institutes of Health, but according to insiders, they don't influence or control the funds for research. Who does wield that power? What are the chances for new paradigm research to be properly recognized?

Candace B. Pert, Ph.D., is the famous graduate student who discovered the opiate receptor on October 25, 1972 and laid the foundation for the discovery of endorphins in 1975. (Endorphins are the body's natural opiate. They suppress pain and produce both euphoria and ecstasy.) As the former chief of brain biochemistry at the National Institutes of Health (NIH) from 1975 to 1987, she became the most cited scientist at one point during her tenure.

Dr. Pert gives us a rare and intimate look at the frustrations of new paradigm research scientists at the mercy of old paradigm medical doctors within the walls of the National Institutes of Health. In her book *Molecules of Emotion,* she exposes the inner workings of the place that puts our tax dollars to work finding "answers to all the big questions of health and disease."[36] As a leading scientist in the field of psychoneuroimmunology, Dr. Pert shares her perspective on the unique research climate at NIH:

> During the thirteen years I spent at the NIH as a research scientist, I referred to the entire conglomerate as the "Palace"...a veritable Versailles, opulently funded with seemingly endless freedom to do research...It seemed as if the old paradigm's insistence on the separation of the mind and body, was as solidly entrenched as the old brick buildings in which the research on those systems took place. Science as an interdisciplinary, interdepartmental phenomenon was an idea whose time had not yet come to the NIH...
>
> The alpha scientists, who had Ph.D. degrees like myself, work for the medical doctors, feeding them data

to present at the many conferences they attend around the globe...No matter how smart or productive he or she may be, the scientist with a Ph.D. has absolutely no chance of ever rising to a position of controlling resources. M.D.s only need apply.[37]

COUNTERACTING THE BAD NEWS

Conscientious scientists, researchers and laypersons across the country are working to change government, medicine and industry in ways that will impact the health of our nation. One of my favorite organizations is the Physicians Committee for Responsible Medicine (PCRM). PCRM continues to provide valuable tools for medical professionals to use in their practices and for lay people to distribute to schools, churches, hospitals and any place in the community where they find an interest in building health and preventing disease.

PCRM explores the role of nutrition in combating specific illnesses, including Alzheimer's disease, arthritis, cancer, high cholesterol levels, diabetes, endometriosis, food-borne illness, heart disease, high blood pressure, mad cow disease, migraines, Parkinson's disease, prostate problems, stroke, premenstrual pain and PMS.

Studies conducted by world-renowned epidemiologists at our leading universities clearly establish the connection between dietary and lifestyle habits and the rate of disease, yet lifestyle issues challenge Americans at every level of society. The natural medical systems have not had a century of visibility to raise the consciousness of our nation. Government agencies charged with promoting dietary guidelines have been tied to business and industrial interests since their inception. As a result, the worst food products—processed, devitalized, chemical-laden, high-fat, high-sugar, low-fiber creations of modern technology—serve as breakfast, lunch and dinner for millions of men, women and children in America.

We need government cooperation with epidemiologists, nutritional biochemists and the work performed at our schools of public health with their new programs in health and fitness. In the absence of visible role models and a national movement supported by all of our institutions to promote healthy dietary and lifestyle habits, we will not overcome the alarming rate of physical, mental and emotional decline in America. Our health is not the priority that it must become to reverse this alarming trend.

What Is a Healthy Lifestyle?

If the American lifestyle is propelling us deeper into a national health crisis, causing people to die of chronic and degenerative diseases that are reversible and preventable, where should we look to observe healthy people?

People living throughout the Pacific Rim, with little or no discretionary income, are among the healthiest people in the world. They consume intact grains (grains that have not been milled or flaked) and vegetables, get less than 10 percent of their protein from animal sources, stay physically active and find satisfaction in meaningful connections with family, extended family and friends. They do not have our diseases and disabilities. It is true after all that the best things in life are free or at least relatively inexpensive.

Most Americans, whether they earn six-figure incomes or rely on food stamps to purchase groceries, do not choose to eat nutritionally dense grains, vegetables and fruits. Instead, they choose the heavily advertised, popular high-fat, high-sugar, chemical-laden, processed, devitalized food. They meet their protein needs by consuming far more than 10 percent of their protein from animal sources. Either they never have been physically active in their lives or they do not remain physically active.

Without following the research-based guidelines developed by other medical systems, conventional, allopathic medicine cannot hope to help patients prevent and overcome multifaceted disorders. The rapidly increasing numbers of people in our country suffering from chronic degenerative conditions threaten the quality of American life and touch everyone in our society.

We cannot resolve this crisis or right the wrongs without understanding and helping the great majority of voting Americans to understand the political, economic, governmental and scientific basis for the current dilemma. We have already lost precious freedoms, including the freedom to choose appropriate medical treatment and healing therapies.

SCIENTIFIC BREAKTHROUGHS CAN HELP

Early twentieth-century pioneers developed natural healing systems based on common sense and intuition. By reclaiming their own health and fitness, they forged a path for millions of people in the first half of the twentieth century. They popularized the therapeutic benefits of an optimal diet (featuring organic whole grains, vegetables and fruits), rigorous physical exercise, pure water and fasting. The

> *Early twentieth-century pioneers developed natural healing systems.*

early health crusaders inspired millions of people by living exemplary lives and modeling their message. They preached sound nutrition, rigorous exercise and faith in God as the way to reverse disease and achieve optimal health.

These activities provided an early twentieth-century application of the new medical paradigm in medicine that would emerge in the last third of the century. Discoveries in the 1970s, particularly in molecular biology, formed the research basis for that new paradigm. These discoveries made in the high-tech biomedical laboratories of the twentieth century show us that what we think and feel, what we eat and what we do with our bodies at every moment alter the body at the molecular level.

These discoveries represent a whole different world of science that contradicts the scientific assumptions of twentieth century biomedicine casting the body as a machine-like mechanism with the functions of the body and mind clearly separated.

WORLD-VIEW: BODY, MIND AND SPIRIT

The current health crisis in America is a result of the old paradigm that separates body and mind. Robert E. Bjork expresses the connection between this outdated world-view and our healthcare crisis in a 1983 journal article:

> Whatever the scope and cause of the medical crisis, many critics believe that much of the problem stems from an outdated world-view based on mechanistic, Cartesian-Newtonian science. Current medical practice is firmly embedded in this conceptual universe, which divides the mind from matter, body from mind.[38]

59

This world-view that embraces the mind-body separation was initiated by Descartes and grew out of the seventeenth-century reality of the established church that claimed all investigations of the mind as strictly their domain.

> ...the Cartesian model initially fit well with the division imposed by the early Church on the mutable body and the immutable soul; the model could allow medical science to move forward, relatively unscathed by attacks from orthodox Christianity.[39]

Again, Candace B. Pert is one of the key researchers whose life work makes it clear that the new paradigm solves the problems that the old paradigm's limited view of health and healing cannot resolve. These exciting discoveries shed light on the functioning of the human body in connection with the mind. She explains the "paradigm-breaking" implications of the research:

> We know that the immune system, like the central nervous system, has memory and the capacity to learn. Thus, it could be said that intelligence is located not only in the brain but in cells that are distributed throughout the body, and that the traditional separation of mental processes, including emotions, from the body is no longer valid.
> If the mind is defined by brain-cell communication, as it has been in contemporary science, then this model of the mind can now be seen as extending naturally to the entire body. Since neuropeptides and their receptors are in the body as well, we may conclude that the mind is in the body, in the same sense that the mind is in the brain, with all that that implies.[40]

Fritjof Capra, Ph.D., a physicist who has written and lectured extensively about the philosophical implications of modern science offered a message, first published in 1982, that desperately needs to be heard and heeded two decades later:

> Medical scientists will have to realize that the reductionist analysis of the body-machine cannot provide them with a complete understanding of human problems.
> ...Many people obstinately adhere to the biomedical model because they are afraid to have their lifestyles

examined and to be confronted with their unhealthy behavior. Rather than face such an embarrassing and often painful situation, they insist on delegating all responsibility for their health to the doctor and the drugs.[41]

UNDENIABLE TESTIMONIALS BIRTH FITNESS BOOM

Paul Bragg, fighting a debilitating bout with tuberculosis as a teenager, made a pledge to God that if he recovered, he would be a crusader for health. He did, and his plan for eating, breathing and exercising served him and millions of others for decades. Dr. Paul Bragg advised Olympic stars, Hollywood stars and industrial giants, and with his daughter Patricia, he ministered to millions through books, tapes, radio and television. Today, Patricia Bragg, N.D., Ph.D., health-food crusader and author, recently established an endowed scholarship for graduate nutrition students at Bastyr University. Paul Bragg ignited a flame in the early twentieth century that has never quit burning.

Jack LaLanne tells another story:

> As a kid I was a sugarholic. I was a junk food junkie! It made me weak and it made me mean. It made me sick. I had boils, pimples and I was nearsighted. Little girls used to beat me up! Mom prayed...the church prayed. At the age of 15 when I heard pioneer nutritionist Paul Bragg speak at the Oakland City Women's Club in the San Francisco bay area, I finally realized that I was addicted to sugar.[42]

Jack attended Paul Bragg's meeting in 1931. Paul Bragg promised Jack LaLanne that if he would exercise and eat a proper diet, he could achieve good health. He found a set of weights at the Berkeley YMCA and began experimenting with them. In 1936, at the age of twenty-one, he opened the first modern health studio on the third floor of an old office building in Oakland, California. Inspired by Paul Bragg, Jack trusted his own instincts and common-sense approach to physical fitness. Rigorous exercise and a healthy diet of natural foods had already become a strange-sounding lifestyle to most people in America in the 1930s. Jack continues his story:

I was 40 years ahead of my time. By then I knew more about the workings of the muscles in my body than most doctors. People thought I was a charlatan and a nut. The doctors were against me—they said that working out with weights would give people heart attacks and they would lose their sex drive; women would look like men. Even the coaches predicted that athletes would get muscle bound and didn't want them to work out with weights. I had to give them keys so they could come in at night and work out. What I was doing was scientifically correct, starting with a healthy diet, and now everyone knows it. Today all the world-class athletes work out with weights.[43]

At age eighty-six, Jack LaLanne makes his daily workouts out a priority. He still lectures and travels all over the world teaching people how to get fit and stay fit. Jack's wife, Elaine, age seventy-one, promotes health and fitness, travels with her husband and lives her message of better living through exercise and nutrition. What an inspiration the LaLannes are for people of every age.

Paul Bragg and Jack LaLanne made a difference. They were decades ahead of the "research" when they listened to their bodies, learned how to restore their health and to prevent chronic disease. No grants. No funding. No billions in research. Just two young men who wanted to get well and stay healthy. So they did—and then they set out to spend the rest of their lives telling other people how to do the same.

In the 1960s, as a U.S. Air Force flight surgeon and director of the Aerospace Medical Laboratory in San Antonio, Dr. Kenneth Cooper became concerned about the lack of physical fitness among the recruits. A graduate of the University of Oklahoma School of Medicine and the Harvard University School of Public Health, Dr. Kenneth Cooper has revolutionized the field of medicine through aerobic exercise. Through his attempt to correct the situation, Dr. Cooper became known as the father of aerobics. He took the adjective *aerobic,* added *s* and coined the word *aerobics.* He developed the 12-minute test and Aerobics Point System that led to his first book, *Aerobics.* When he wrote the book in 1968, a potential publisher told him that no one would buy a book with such an obscure title.

The book sold millions of copies, and a young doctor from Oklahoma soon received recognition as a visionary. He became a leader in the field we now know as preventive medicine. With that book, many believe, he ushered in the fitness boom. The National Center for Chronic Disease Prevention and Health Promotion would agree. Today many U.S. and foreign corporations, more than 2,500 universities and public schools, as well as the Army, Navy and Secret Service utilize his program. Now, seventy-plus years old and enjoying five full-time jobs, Dr. Cooper still lives a great and balanced life. In 1982, *The London Times* named Dr. Cooper among the top seventy-five greatest people in the world during the last twenty years.

When Kenneth Cooper left the military to set up a preventive medical practice in Dallas, Texas, against the advice of nearly everyone, he faced ridicule, hostility and serious opposition. The Texas Medical Association had no admiration for a young doctor who believed that post-coronary patients should be put on monitored exercise programs. Experts warned him that people would die and that he would be putting his career as a doctor, as well as the lives of his patients, in jeopardy.

Cooper proceeded with his plans and began systematically collecting data that would one day reveal that movement does not impede the recovery from a heart attack; rather, a lack of movement places the post-coronary patient in peril. In those days, physicians still prescribed bed rest for coronary patients, which is today recognized as a perilous protocol.

Approaching his seventieth year, Dr. Cooper had this to say about the challenges in his life:

> I've had the privilege of founding and building an internationally recognized preventive medicine health center, which has provided many people with life-enhancing, and sometimes life-saving, healthcare... The stress has been almost unbearable at times. I tell my friends to look into my face and see the deep furrow and grooves imbedded there. Those lines were earned in hand-to-hand combat on the front lines of many medical and business battlefields.
>
> Over the years I've fought to put the Cooper Aerobics Center, Clinic, and Institute for Aerobics

Research on a firm professional and financial footing. I've dueled with opponents on scientific issues ranging from the usefulness of exercise to the value of antioxidants. And I've agonized over whether, or how far to expand our operations and expertise to other locales and venues.[44]

In 2000, Dr. Cooper, founder and president of the world-renowned Cooper Aerobic Center in Dallas, Texas, celebrated its thirtieth anniversary. His message remains clear: "It is easier to maintain good health through proper exercise, diet and emotional balance than it is to regain it once it is lost."[45]

Just like the many biomedical physicians, scientists, leaders of various natural healing systems and nonphysician health practitioners, Kenneth Cooper was decades ahead of the research. Like them, he followed the counsel of his own conscience, genius and wisdom within in his soul. He listened to his own body, learned how to restore health and to prevent chronic disease. And just like the pioneers in health and fitness before him, he had no billions of dollars in research grants. As a young man, Kenneth Cooper decided he wanted to be strong and well. So he achieved that goal, and then he set out to spend the rest of his life helping others do the same.

The medical establishment and our government have ignored efforts made throughout the twentieth century by such eminent scientists, experienced and able medical doctors from many healing systems and gifted nonphysician practitioners with expertise in a wide range of healing therapies.

Fritjof Capra, addressing the dangers of the old paradigm, comments on the challenges most apparent during the 1980s:

> The biomedical model today is much more than a model. Among the medical profession it has acquired the status of dogma, and for the general public it is inextricably linked to the common cultural belief system. To go beyond it will require nothing less than a profound cultural revolution. And such a revolution is necessary if we want to improve, or even maintain, our health. The shortcomings of our current healthcare system—in terms of health costs, effectiveness, and fulfillment of

64

human needs—are becoming more and more conspicuous and are increasingly recognized as stemming from the restrictive nature of the conceptual model on which it is based.[46]

RESTORING OUR PRECIOUS FREEDOMS

I believe that we are clearly experiencing a scientific revolution. We can hope that the current health and healing crisis, as well as the increasing adversity in an ever more dangerous world, will prompt "awakenings" throughout the culture. Some will be spiritual awakenings and others intellectual awakenings. I believe that in the difficult times ahead, many people will seek to know God. As we awaken to the

> *We are clearly experiencing a scientific revolution.*

political realities and to the realities of our own physical, mental, emotional and spiritual needs, we will seek creative ways to bring better health, healthcare and true healing—body, mind and spirit—to our land.

As voters, we need to unite in an unprecedented nonpartisan way and no longer tolerate the existing laws, regulations and bureaucratic policies denying us medical freedom. If we don't come together, we as patients will lose our freedom to choose appropriate care, and the health practitioners' right to provide that appropriate care will continue to diminish. Together, we have the power to win back the freedom that each of us wants and needs in order to prevent and overcome the diseases that are afflicting our nation.

The medical-pharmaceutical-industrial-governmental alliance devours our tax dollars to satisfy business and industrial interests rather than provide real solutions for our health problems. If we are denied access to the full range of natural medical systems, healing therapies and related goods and services, then we are robbed of the right to make our best effort to get well and to overcome debilitating, chronic diseases.

If biomedicine is allowed to continue impeding the development, progress and practice of other medical systems in the

United States, how can we possibly regard ourselves as a government of the people, by the people and for the people? If our right to choose nontoxic, noninvasive medical systems and healing therapies is not an integral part of the right to life, liberty and the pursuit of happiness, we have to wonder what constitutes the right to life, liberty and the pursuit of happiness.

Food and beverage manufacturers in this country produce most of the items that people eat and drink for breakfast, lunch, dinner, dessert, snacks and recreation. These privately owned companies operate for profit with the goal of becoming wealthy in a competitive market. That is capitalism. As consumers, we are free to choose what we wish to buy or what we do not wish to buy. Most consumers do not understand how the industrial-governmental alliance works against them. The larger the company, the more governmental control is exercised, and thus, huge amounts of money are spent to make sure that the public stays confused.

In a free market economy, we certainly don't deny individuals, business and industry the right to produce and sell an infinite number and variety of products (many of which may be reprehensible and repugnant to other Americans) and the legal right of all Americans to buy those products. We regularly buy and sell products and services that reasonable people find threatening, harmful and destructive to the physical, mental, emotional and spiritual health of millions of people. People choose what to produce, what to market and what to consume—based on their personal world-views, lifestyle, moral and religious values, social-economic-educational-environmental influences and personal codes of ethics and conduct.

How, in the rough and tumble of what we have come to prize as freedom, did we ever let go of the right to choose our own health practitioners? How could we lose the right of all of the healing arts and medical systems to offer treatments, therapies and counsel to every man, woman and child in America?

Enlightened and active consumers bent on being good neighbors and reeducating each other can make the "government of the people, by the people and for the people" actually happen. Elected representatives begin to remember who we are and why we matter—when they hear from us. A consumer movement of this magnitude could be called a revolutionary change, but I still think that an awakening is what will be required.

Most of the people who represent us in Congress also want to protect vital freedoms, promote health and disease prevention, stop wasting trillions of dollars funding treatments that don't work in reversing chronic conditions and begin funding treatments that do. They are just waiting to hear from an enlightened and determined electorate. Then they too will experience "an awakening." We need to find in ourselves, and inspire in others, the will to be well, to be free, and to be of service to those who are not able to fight this battle for themselves.

Medical-pharmaceutical-industrial interests currently have the money and power to delay progress on all legislation related to health and healthcare because we have not arisen as a nation to stop those interests with our voices and our votes. Consumer groups like those I have listed that are seeking to win back and to protect medical freedom are a precious resource:

- American Association for Health Freedom (www.ampa.net)

- California Citizens for Health Freedom (www.citizenshealth.org)

- Foundation for the Advancement of Innovative Medicine (www.faim.org)

- Minnesota Natural Health Coalition (www.minnesotanatualhealth.org).

These are only a few of the groups trying to preserve and win back freedom of consumers to access, and health practitioners to provide, nontoxic, noninvasive natural treatment for the prevention and cure of disease.

In the face of ridicule throughout the1960s (by those promoting a better life through chemistry), a pluralistic healing system remained alive, but it was thwarted at every turn by our medical monopoly. As a result, three decades later, getting treatment for allergies, asthma, ADHD or any other chronic condition means, for many people, finding the right medication to suppress symptoms—not getting well and actually overcoming the condition. As drugs suppress the symptoms, the body gets weaker, and the chronic conditions become worse. Drugs are used, not to heal diseases, but to manage them. Over time, sick patients just get sicker. That's where we are.

We have new-paradigm scientists, physicians and educators eager to develop methods and materials for teaching every man, woman and child in America how to prevent and overcome chronic degenerative conditions. Among these courageous warriors, there are shining examples of how genuine science, based on decades of solid research, can win out over business interests that clearly promote disease and death.

When our government begins funding dietary and lifestyle guidelines based on the research studies, then that will be a leap forward. Popularizing the dietary habits that clearly build, maintain and restore health and delivering the clearest warnings possible to consumers regarding products, goods and services that undermine health, will cause consumer spending to change. Consumer interests will be served.

However, when the United States Department of Agriculture, supported by our tax dollars, popularizes categories of food (based on business interests) through educational programs (e.g., the USDA Food Pyramid and all previous USDA dietary guidelines), they violate a sacred trust. They betray the people who believe the guidelines are scientific. Average Americans, busy with their jobs and children, can't make any sense out of a few isolated negative reports they hear through the print or electronic media, criticizing governmental guidelines. Why should they believe the university scientists who say that the guidelines are not based on epidemiological studies, or any kind of studies, when the government has its own scientists? Why would the government promote information that would undermine the nation's health?

Our awakening has been slow and plodding. Few saw a health crisis in the making in the 1950s or 1960s. Our institutions supported the notion of a better world through chemistry. The sixties' "establishment" considered health and fitness buffs eccentric. They viewed health food stores as havens for longhaired hippies and granola people, or as businesses operated by people they considered misguided and unenlightened health enthusiasts (e.g., natural hygienists and Seventh-Day Adventists). However, the truth surfaced in the second half of the twentieth century. As it turned out, research confirmed the effectiveness of the recommendations made by many of the "misguided and unenlightened." The changes have been slow in coming, and the victories were hard won.

RESPONSE TO SUDDEN CRISIS

Sudden crisis evokes a different response than do daily difficulties. In the aftermath of an unexpected calamity, our very souls are awakened to who we are and who we are not. Most importantly, we are awakened, by the grace of God, to who we can become.

For our nation, September 11, 2001 came upon us like a movie nightmare. No one could have ever fathomed the devastation that unfolded before our very eyes. Many of us sat motionless before television screens, helpless as the strange, dark force killed, maimed and devastated everything in its path. The survivors of the attack, and the world outside that deadly pathway, were too stunned by death

Few saw a health crisis in the making in the 1950s or 1960s.

and debris to fathom the endless cascade of meaning that would bombard us, consciously and unconsciously, for months.

Then, came a new dawning, a fresh revelation: We have hope. We found that hope in the people who serve us—policemen and firefighters, in the people who wander into our lives from all walks of life, willing to give their lives, risk all that they hold dear, to save the lives of strangers—to save one of us. What we saw of heroism in downtown Manhattan made us feel proud of America and, through a deep and empathetic connection, made us feel good about ourselves. The grace that caused ordinary people to become extraordinary heroes gave us hope that we too possess the potential for great mercy, great wisdom and great love.

> I command you to love each other in the same way that I love you. And here is how to measure it—the greatest love is shown when people lay down their lives for their friends.
>
> **—JOHN 15:12–13**

Now, we are awakening to an equally unimaginable crisis in our nation. It is the reality that millions of Americans are dying or disabled as a result of preventable, and often reversible, diseases. We are spending vast amounts of money for treating these chronic diseases in the most ineffective ways. We don't know if we have been simply ignorant or if we have just been so cowardly, unimpassioned and absorbed with our own self-interests that we couldn't imagine taking a stand against the Goliath of modern-day medicine.

This hideous crisis did not traumatize us as much as the 9-11 tragedy. Most ignored the quiet revolt from the fifties through the nineties. Most denied its existence. We, the richest nation in the world, and in many ways most blessed, have made choices that have impoverished our lives. At every socioeconomic level, we have cultivated tastes for activities that make us weak and foods that cause disease. All the while, we are not mindful, nor in awe, of the people on the other side of the globe who eat, sleep, work and play differently than we do—and who don't have most of our diseases.

Now we need to shake ourselves and awaken to who we are and who we are not. We are a people overcome by diseases of our own making. We are not the healthiest people in the world, and we are not the wisest. But, we can overcome this crisis by His grace and become whole. We can learn to see, hear, taste, smell and touch the miracles around us as we drink from the fountain of life.

THE BEST AND WORST OF TIMES

It is the best and the worst of times for growing up and growing old in America. We have unprecedented opportunities in this twenty-first century to prosper physically, mentally, emotionally and spiritually, but we must do so in the midst of a world going mad from its own excess.

At times when we are in a medical crisis—as a result of accidents, injuries or the acute stages of chronic disease—we will be grateful that biomedical intervention can save and extend our lives. We will remember that our lives would be different if we were living in a Third World country during such an emergency. We will seek biomedical solutions (across a vast array of medical specialties) when a crisis warrants that particular expertise.

However, we must develop an understanding of what constitutes appropriate self-care, so that preventing disease, maintaining health and restoring our bodies become a moment-by-moment habit that engages us physically, mentally, emotionally and spiritually. As we acquire knowledge of natural healing systems and traditional medicine, we prepare ourselves for the time when we may need to choose physicians and non-physician practitioners who can help us overcome conditions that we are not able to treat on our own.

> *It is the best and worst of times for growing up and growing old in America.*

We live in a culture that often grabs at everything, savoring little or nothing. By embracing perversions in every sensual pleasure, we are a nation that has lost the knowledge, joy, wonder and ecstasy of walking in the abundance of God's provision—real food, pure air and water, quietness, fertile soil, plants and animals, geological wonders, every breath of life and, most of all, His Holy Spirit to guide and comfort us.

A common-sense quest to reclaim lost knowledge propelled a twentieth-century movement that began in the 1930s, took hold in the 1950s and 1960s and has resulted in the twenty-first-century explosion of health-related goods, services and information. Now the challenge is to sift, to discern, to grasp the essentials, to learn and to teach others how to become healthy and whole. A basic understanding of how we heal will help us to sort out what we need to do to enjoy total health and restoration.

Part Three
How We Heal

KEY HEALTH ISSUES

Making Foods Your Medicine

Balancing Your Hormones

The Spiritual Connection

Exercise Needed to Restore Your Body, Mind and Spirit

How We Heal

Making Foods Your Medicine

KEY QUESTIONS:

1. **W**HAT CAN WE LEARN FROM THE HEALTHIEST PEOPLE IN THE WORLD?

2. **W**HAT WHOLE FOODS AND DIETARY REGIMENS HAVE THE POWER TO REVERSE CHRONIC CONDITIONS?

3. **W**HY IS INSULIN SENSITIVITY AN IMPORTANT MARKER FOR LIFE SPAN?

Hippocrates lived four centuries before Christ, and many people still consider him the father of medicine. Hippocrates taught that "nature is the healer of all diseases." He advised that food must become our medicine and medicine our food.[1] In our twenty-first-century world, we can still observe people groups and entire cultures that thrive on natural foods and enjoy optimum health living close to nature. They have escaped the degenerative diseases and chronic conditions that plague their more civilized and highly developed neighbor societies.

THE HEALTHIEST PEOPLE IN THE WORLD

Where do the healthiest people in the world live? What do they eat? How much time do they spend doing physical activities? Answering these simple questions can help us to contrast their healthy lifestyles with dietary and lifestyle choices we have made as individuals and as a nation that have resulted in the inevitable consequences of chronic and degenerative disease.

MEDITERRANEAN PEOPLES OF THE 1960s

The adult life expectancy in Crete, much of the rest of Greece and southern Italy in the early 1960s was among the highest in the world. Their rates of coronary heart disease, certain cancers and other diet-related chronic diseases were among the lowest in the world.[2] These cultures' health and longevity are especially significant in light of the limitations in existing medical services in the region at that time. Epidemiologists and nutritionists have studied the lifetime dietary habits of the people living in this region to discover their secrets.

Dr. Walter Willett is one of the authors of the "Mediterranean Diet Pyramid: A Cultural Model for Healthy Eating." He also helped Oldways Preservation and Trust to create a series of food pyramids based on traditional diets—including the Mediterranean Pyramid. These pyramids offer important information on the positive health benefits of various traditional dietary regimens. The main characteristics of the Mediterranean diet of the 1960s follow:

- They consumed an abundance of food from plant sources, including fruits and vegetables, potatoes, breads and grains, beans, nuts and seeds.

- Their diet emphasized a variety of minimally processed and, wherever possible, seasonally fresh and locally grown foods (which often maximizes the health-promoting micronutrient and antioxidant content of these foods).

- They used crude extra-virgin olive oil as the principal fat, replacing other fats and oils (including butter and margarine).

- Their total fat consumption ranged from less than 25 percent to over 35 percent of energy (calories), with saturated fat no more than 7 to 8 percent of energy (calories).

- They consumed daily portions, in low to moderate amounts, of cheese and yogurt.

- They consumed weekly portions of moderate amounts of fish and poultry. Several times a month they ate red meat.

- They consumed from zero to four eggs per week (including those used in cooking and baking).

- They participated in regular physical activity at levels that promote a healthy weight, fitness and well-being.

- They consumed moderate amounts of wine, normally with meals, about one to two glasses per day for men and one glass per day for women.

THE RURAL CHINESE PEOPLES

An elaborate study of the lives of rural Chinese people revealed that they are among the healthiest people in China and in the world. Some of the important findings of the China-Cornell-Oxford Diet and Health Project are:

- The healthiest people in China get only 7 to 10 percent

of their protein from animal sources (meat, fish, poultry, eggs and dairy).

- ❧ A dietary regimen high in complex carbohydrates and low in fat (as opposed to our American regimen high in refined carbohydrates, low in fiber and high in fat) enables people to consume significantly more calories without gaining weight.

- ❧ The Chinese do not suffer from iron deficiency while consuming plant-based regimens, nor do they suffer (as do many Americans) from iron overload.

- ❧ The Chinese drastically reduce the likelihood of osteoporosis by limiting foods that are high in phosphates (e.g., meat, poultry, fish and dairy).

CHARACTERISTICS OF HEALTHY CULTURES

Epidemiological studies reveal that cultures that represent the healthiest people alive today have much in common with each other. Their life-extending habits are simple for us to embrace, if we have the will to do so. For example, the rural Chinese eat an abundance of intact grain (i.e., grain before it is milled or flaked). Many people living in primitive cultures consume very simple foods—grains, vegetables, beans and little or no refined carbohydrates. They are not predominantly vegetarians. However, they do not gorge themselves on animal products as do people in Western cultures.

These cultures consider their lifestyles eventful and their foods palatable. In spite of the fact that they have relatively few food choices, their meals are festive, communal and physically satisfying. Their cuisine provides them with physical stamina as well. Men and women in these societies live vigorous mental and physical lives well beyond the age of ninety.

In contrast, many Americans who have reached midlife begin seeking solutions to brain fog, short-term memory loss and a wide range of life-threatening diseases. We pay a high price for a diet characterized by processed devitalized carbohydrates: processed foods filled with sugar and the worst fats and chemicals. Every day millions of people in America stand in grocery store and supermarket checkout lines exchanging years of their lives, along with the quality of their lives, for packaged trash— and they pay money to do it.

To summarize the characteristics of the healthiest cultures in the world, the chart below lists the simple dietary regimen they follow that gives them a long life and a quality of life few Americans can expect to enjoy.

CHARACTERISTICS OF HEALTHY CULTURES

- They eat an abundance of plant-based foods.
- They consume minimally processed, seasonally fresh, locally grown foods.
- They consume little or no saturated fat.
- They consume few or no sweets.
- They eat an abundance of dietary fiber.

TWO UNIVERSAL PRINCIPLES

If an individual is seeking to enjoy a better quality of life, then he simply needs to observe two universal principles. The first universal principle of healthy dietary regimens is that *healthy people don't eat refined carbohydrates*. Refined carbohydrates lead to obesity and chronic disease. Eating whole foods, real food, is the basis for optimal health.

The second universal principle regarding a healthy lifestyle is

---

Healthy people don't eat refined carbohydrates.

---

that *healthy people are involved in daily, rigorous, physical activity*. People who continue to build muscle, remain flexible and exercise aerobically during the routine course of living are among the healthiest people in the world.

COMPARING LEVELS OF DIETARY FAT

Most Americans are aware of the controversy surrounding our culture's low-fat diet scenario that promises weight loss and protection against certain diseases. It is interesting to note that between two of the most significant groups of healthy cultures in the world, the rural Chinese and the Mediterranean peoples of the 1960s, their fat intakes vary widely:

- People in rural China consume a diet that is extremely low in fat. They get 7 to 10 percent of their protein from animal sources (fish, poultry, eggs and dairy). Those who are genetically predisposed are at risk for disease when they consume even small amounts of animal protein.

- The Mediterranean peoples in the early 1960s—in Crete, much of the rest of Greece and southern Italy— reflected a total fat consumption of 25 to over 35 percent of energy (calories), with saturated fat no more than 7–8 percent of energy (calories). They used crude extra-virgin olive oil as the principal fat, replacing other fats and oils (including butter and margarine). Extra-virgin olive oil is a monounsaturated fat.

It is the *type* of fat that is the most significant factor in reversing chronic degenerative disease. Cells' membranes require omega-3 fatty acid derivatives (EPA and DHA) for fluidity. Monounsaturated fats found in nuts and extra-virgin olive oil balance the fluidity in the cells' membranes. Too much omega-3 would have an oxidizing (disease-causing) effect on the cell. These healthy monounsaturated fats and vitamin E prevent that from happening.

Our bodies are able to manufacture these omega-3 derivatives from vegetarian sources, particularly green foods when we are healthy. The elderly and people on drugs or in a weakened state may not be able to make enough omega-3 derivatives. In those cases, we must consume the omega-3 fatty acids directly from animal sources by eating cold-water fish such as salmon, mackerel, tuna and sardines, as well as grass-fed beef.

When we store excess fat in our bodies, we store mostly saturated fat. Grain-fed beef that dominates the beef market in the United States is high in saturated fat. The organic grass-fed beef that is now available in some markets has not been injected with hormones, does not contain pesticides and is high in omega-3 fatty acids.

The Mediterranean diet of the 1960s, high in monounsaturated fats, offers enormous health benefits. And it convincingly proves, in comparison with the Chinese low-fat consumption, that it is the type of fats, rather than the quantity of fat, that is the distinguishing feature in healthy diets.

POOR FAT SOURCES

When we consume excessive amounts of carbohydrates (especially the processed, devitalized no-fiber varieties), we end up with a diet that produces saturated fat. Even though we are consuming zero-saturated fat from animal sources and are following a low-fat diet, we are storing saturated fat from our high-carbohydrate intake.

Eating excessive amounts of "junk" carbohydrates is the single deadliest feature of the American diet. Everything from devitalized grains to sugary soda and candy, foods that are not real foods at all are the products Americans crave most. Yet, they are advertised as "fat-free" items in order to convince us that we should include them in our low-fat diets. This is one of the reasons we have become a nation of sick people who are getting sicker.

At the other extreme, a high-protein diet can be equally as harmful as a high-carbohydrate diet. We need adequate protein, but too much protein also makes us sick. Physical activity does have a bearing on the amount of protein the body requires. If we consume more protein than we require daily, it is converted to body fat when our energy requirements have already been met by other dietary components.

A HEALTHY FOOD PYRAMID

Dr. Walter Willett, M.D., chairman of the Department of Nutrition at Harvard School of Public Health, and his colleagues constructed Willett's Healthy Eating Pyramid, a new healthy pyramid designed to replace (and expose the dangers of) the United States Department of Agriculture's Food Guide Pyramid.[4] The foundation of Dr. Willett's Healthy Eating Pyramid is exercise, supporting the fact that physical activity is one of the primary determinants of health. On the second level, he promotes whole grains and healthy fats. The research concerning effective ways to prevent and overcome chronic degenerative disease is conclusive: *Food can heal our bodies.* The following concepts are an essential part of any optimal dietary regimen.

- Plant-based (high-fiber, whole foods) regimens prevent and cure degenerative disease.

- Appropriate amounts of intact grains (e.g., wheat, barley, oats, quinoa, buckwheat and rice before they are milled or flaked) strengthen the body and help stabilize blood sugar levels.

- Non-glutinous grains (quinoa, millet, amaranth, buckwheat and rice) should replace glutinous grains (e.g., wheat, barley, oats and rye) in the diets of many people in Western cultures who suffer from gluten intolerance and gluten sensitivities. Eliminating glutinous grains is often extremely beneficial for people suffering from chronic disease.

- Enzyme-rich raw vegetables and fruits contain antioxidants, phytochemicals and insoluble fiber that protect, restore and revitalize the body.

- Omega-3 and omega-6 essential fatty acids are vital for the optimal function of virtually every system in the body. Modern diets are drastically lacking (some completely lacking) in omega-3 fatty acids in particular.

People in other parts of the world who have never studied health and nutrition do achieve optimal health. Each generation passes along wisdom concerning the healthful and healing dietary regimens they have practiced. We have lost our way in America. Processed foods and soft drinks earn manufacturers billions of dollars in revenue. Our entire culture is addicted to these products. We now crave an abundance of deadly foods that dominate the supermarkets and restaurants across America.

As Americans, living in a culture of chronic disease, we tend to lose sight of the fact that we were not always a nation of very sick people. The following chart summarizes the stark reality of what we have become as a nation.

Facts of Our Culture

- More than 90 million Americans live with chronic illnesses.

- Chronic diseases account for 70 percent of all deaths in the United States.

- The medical care costs of people with chronic diseases account for more than 60 percent of the nation's medical care costs.

- Chronic diseases account for one-third of the years of potential life lost before age sixty-five.[5]

Obesity and Overweight

Recent results of the 1999 National Health and Nutrition Examination Survey (NHANES) indicate that obesity and overweight are a national epidemic. According to the survey, an estimated 61 percent of U.S. adults are either overweight or obese, defined as having a body mass index (BMI) of 25 or more. The percentage of children and adolescents who are defined as overweight has more than doubled since the early 1970s. About 13 percent of children and adolescents are now seriously overweight.

In spite of the public health impact of obesity and overweight, these conditions have not been a major public health priority in the past. These experts agree that halting and reversing the upward trend of the obesity epidemic will require effective collaboration among government, voluntary and private sectors, as well as a commitment to action by individuals and communities across the nation.[6]

Overweight and obese individuals (BMI of 25 and above) are at increased risk for the following physical ailments:

HEALTH RISKS OF OBESITY

- High blood pressure, hypertension
- High blood cholesterol, dyslipidemia
- Type 2 (non-insulin dependent) diabetes
- Insulin resistance, glucose intolerance
- Hyperinsulinemia
- Coronary heart disease
- Angina pectoris
- Congestive heart failure
- Stroke
- Gallstones
- Cholescystitis and cholelithiasis
- Gout
- Osteoarthritis
- Obstructive sleep apnea and respiratory problems
- Some types of cancer (such as endometrial, breast, prostate and colon)
- Complications of pregnancy
- Poor female reproductive health (such as menstrual irregularities, infertility, irregular ovulation)
- Bladder control problems (such as stress incontinence)
- Uric acid nephrolithiasis
- Psychological disorders such as depression, eating disorders, distorted body image and low self-esteem.[7]

Many people have spent their lives taking drugs to suppress the symptoms. For those struggling with overweight and obesity, changing dietary habits, even for those who are highly motivated, presents challenges. The reality is that after eating high-fat, devitalized, chemical-laden foods, filled with trans-fatty acids, artificial flavors, artificial colors and sugar—a great number of adults and children develop food allergies and food sensitivities to pure, nutritionally dense whole foods.

Physician and nonphysician health practitioners can help by providing simple tests for diagnosing food intolerances, food allergies and food sensitivities. There is hope for reversing even the most stubborn cases of obesity through nutritional and dietary regimens.

CHRONIC DISEASE IN CHILDREN

One of the more appalling facets of the health crisis today in the United States is the fact that our children are developing a wide range of chronic conditions, including Type 2 diabetes and serious autoimmune disorders. An entire generation is at risk of developing a variety of chronic degenerative diseases because of our poor dietary and lifestyle habits.

TRAGIC COST OF DIABETES

- Seventeen million Americans have diabetes, and 16 million more have a condition that is now called "pre-diabetes."

- Hispanics and African Americans are almost twice as likely as whites to have diabetes.

- Diabetes is the fifth leading cause of death by disease. More than 200,000 Americans die from diabetes each year. In the next decade, researchers expect more than two million Americans will die from diabetes.

- Diabetes increases the risk of heart disease and stroke two to four times, and is the leading cause of adult blindness, amputations and kidney failure.

- Life expectancy of people with diabetes is ten to fifteen years less than for the general population. Death rates are twice as high among middle-aged people with diabetes as among middle-aged people without diabetes. People with diabetes have the same cardiovascular risk as those who have already had a heart attack.

- Diabetes costs the country $100 billion annually.

- Twenty-five percent of Medicare expenditures go to care for people with diabetes.

- The Center for Disease Control and Prevention calls diabetes an "epidemic." The prevalence of diabetes in the United States population has increased by 50 percent since 1990. At the current rate of growth, more than 10 percent of Americans will have diabetes in ten years.

- In 1999, the congressionally mandated, NIH-appointed Diabetes Research Working Group (DRWG) recognized "both great urgency and unprecedented opportunities in diabetes research...The DRWG has identified five areas that offer extraordinary opportunities for making genuine and significant progress toward understanding, more effectively treating, and ultimately preventing and curing diabetes. They are: autoimmunity and the beta cell; cell signaling and cell regulation; obesity; and clinical research and clinical trials of critical importance."[8]

By treating *symptoms* of chronic disease, instead of focusing on the underlying *causes* of chronic disease (the approach of allopathic medicine), the result is that we prolong and often exacerbate chronic disorders. Another result of this approach can be the actual development of additional chronic diseases.

OVER-THE-COUNTER REMEDIES

Keeping a cabinet full of drugs to remedy the symptoms of disease when we get sick has become an acceptable way of life in our country.

Hours of advertisements on radio and television feature prescription and nonprescription treatments for indigestion, heartburn, acid reflux, constipation, hemorrhoids, erectile dysfunction, overactive bladder, diarrhea, headaches, PMS, migraines, sinus attacks, allergies, colds, flu, depression, high blood pressure and high cholesterol. The people in the ads all look nice. They look like people we know; they look like us. We conclude that somebody we know must surely be buying this stuff; it is probably OK for us, too.

Ron Rosedale, M.D., an expert in antiaging medicine and effective nutritional treatments for diabetes and other chronic diseases, tells about his experiences with patients during the ten years he spent specializing in ear, nose and throat medicine. Patients—many, many patients—came to him after their family doctors treated their colds by giving them Sudafed. Subsequent to taking the decongestant they developed sinus infections and decided to visit an ear, nose and throat specialist. Why did they need the attention of a specialist at this stage?

The decongestant Sudafed had shut down the mucus. However, that mucus contains a very strong antibody to kill the virus (secretory IgA). Decongestants constrict the blood vessels and dam up the constant stream of mucus with its healing properties. When we shut down the natural healing system of the body to treat symptoms, we usually make the disease worse.

THE IMPACT OF DIET

If physicians would dedicate themselves to understanding the tremendous impact that diet and lifestyle have on our bodies, we would see a wonderful paradigm shift in our medical establishment that would begin to turn the tide of our national health crisis. As individuals, we need to recognize the powerful effects—for good or ill—of everything we choose to eat.

Some people may discover that the variety of symptoms they are suffering are aggravated by certain foods. They may have developed food allergies or food intolerances. If so, they can learn to rely on the whole foods and whole-food concentrates that offer specific relief for their symptoms while providing an ideal supply of micronutrients and phytochemicals. It is time to regard food as medicine.

When we look at the healing power of food on a person-by-person basis, we recognize that our genetic predispositions and biochemical individuality account for much of the variety in our responses. One person may succumb to a particular disease, while another person with the same poor dietary and lifestyle habits develops a different chronic condition or experiences the symptoms of chronic disease much later in life. Each of us faces a different set of challenges in response to the same poor dietary and lifestyle choices.

It is time to regard food as medicine.

Regenerating Power of Natural Therapies

Dietary and nutritional therapies offer strategies for regenerating the systems in the body (e.g., the digestive, immune, endocrine and cardiovascular systems) so that they will work well again. Micronutrients and macronutrients have variable effects on each of us depending upon our unique physical, mental and emotional characteristics. The quantity of micronutrients (vitamins, minerals and amino acids) that we require in overcoming chronic disease and the optimal balance of macronutrients (proteins, carbohydrates and fats) that produces healing effects differ for each of us. These are discoveries we make as we learn to pay attention to our bodies and seek optimal health.

Phytochemicals, plant chemicals that contribute to the bright colors of fruits and vegetables, also have an amazing impact on human health and nutrition. In regarding food as medicine, we will need to learn to consume valuable phytochemicals from food sources (as opposed to nutritional supplements) to enjoy their full effect on optimal health and nutrition.

The good news is we can overcome genetic predispositions. Using food and exercise as therapy (instead of drugs that suppress symptoms), we can safely discover our peculiar micronutrient and macronutrient needs. Only then will we avoid the diet dilemma and embark on a path to optimal health and weight.

Immediate Relief Available

After years of debilitating dietary and lifestyle habits, using food as therapy often gives us immediate relief from some symptoms and maximizes our ability to completely overcome chronic disease. While experiencing symptoms of chronic disease, however, many people are often limited in the *type and amounts* of whole foods they can tolerate, such as fiber, intact grains and fruit. Once the body responds to these whole foods and our systems are functioning optimally, then we can begin to consume a greater variety of nutritious whole foods.

As we continue to monitor our progress on the health continuum through appropriate diagnostic tests, we can verify that we are still on track. The pleasure found in newly acquired tastes for delicious whole-foods cuisine, and the experience of physical, mental and emotional health and well-being, are powerful rewards for abandoning destructive dietary and lifestyle habits.

RECOGNIZING YOUR FOOD ALLERGIES

Before you opt out of the suggestion of eating natural, whole foods for health with, *You don't understand; those kinds of foods make me sick!,* please read on. It is true that the reality of food allergies may make you react negatively to some foods. It is important for you to understand how to identify any allergies you may have and then learn to eat the whole foods that you can tolerate.

Two different kinds of allergic reactions exist. The first type is often referred to as the *fixed allergy.* It produces hives, swelling, congestion or life-threatening anaphylaxis hours or even minutes after eating a food to which you are allergic. Conventional biomedical allergists, as well as alternative allergists, are able to diagnose fixed food allergies through various testing methods.

A very different kind of food allergy concerns us as we plan a therapeutic dietary regimen for people who are suffering from chronic multifaceted degenerative diseases. It is a *delayed allergy,* also referred to as cyclic, masked or hidden food allergy. Delayed, or hidden, food allergies are controversial within biomedical circles because they defy the biomedical model in which "diseases are treated as universal entities rather than as individual afflictions different for everyone."[9] Symptoms of hidden food allergies may include hundreds of symptoms that accompany other chronic diseases. Does everyone have hidden food allergies, sensitivities or intolerances? No, but James Braley, M.D. predicts the following regarding hidden food allergies:

> Seventy to 80 percent of Americans currently suffering from chronic medical conditions of unknown cause, who have proven poorly responsive to conventional medical interventions, are suffering...delayed-onset food allergies.[10]

He goes on to say that medical research has linked delayed food allergies to over 150 chronic conditions, including the following common conditions:[11]

COMMON CHRONIC CONDITIONS

Asthma	Type 2 diabetes
Arthritis	Middle ear infections
ADD/ADHD	Autism
Leaky gut syndrome	Migraine headaches
Candidiasis	Hyperactivity
Celiac disease	Hypoglycemia
Chronic fatigue	Hypertension
Depression	Anxiety
Bedwetting	Bone and muscle pain
Fluid in middle ear	Irritable bowel syndrome
Fibromyalgia	Cluster headaches
Skin rashes	Sinusitis
Weight gain	Panic attacks
Crohn's disease	

ARE YOU ALLERGIC TO BREAD?

True food allergies occur when the immune system reacts to a protein (i.e., allergen) from a particular food. The body's reaction to this protein, or allergen, causes the immune system to attack the "foreign" substance. Gluten is the protein in wheat and other grains that causes the main problem for people who experience allergic reactions to them.

Diseases that occur in response to the proteins in wheat (called celiac disease) are second only to the diseases related to the consumption of milk (lactose intolerance). Experts once considered celiac disease to be a rare occurrence, but now with the appropriate screening tests widely available, research reveals that celiac disease is common.

> Many people who have the disease, especially children, don't have the classic gastrointestinal symptoms that have commonly signaled the condition. In some cases, there are no symptoms at all. These people have "silent celiac disease"; the damage to the small intestine is prevalent but without obvious symptoms.[12]

Many people go for decades without a diagnosis of celiac disease while serious complications develop. Anemia, osteoporosis or autoimmune disease may be the first symptoms of celiac disease that a patient develops. According to recent studies, it may affect the brain as well. Debilitating headaches have been dramatically reduced in some patients when they eliminated gluten from their diets.[13]

Melissa Diane Smith, a nutritionist and health journalist based in Tucson, Arizona, offers examples from the cases of three women, who after years suffering from various problems, were eventually diagnosed with gluten sensitivities.

> Yvonne Gifford experienced exhaustion for 20 years... Mary Thorpe had a history of canker sores, migraine headaches and depression since her late teens, then developed digestive problems and itchy blisters on her legs a few years ago...Barbara Schneider suffered through frequent stomach distention for decades...she developed chronic diarrhea.[14]

The good news is that it is not difficult to treat the cause of celiac disease or other hidden allergies. Once it's diagnosed, eliminating the offending allergens from the diet can bring dramatic results for the sufferer. A gluten-free diet can bring great relief to those whose immune system cannot tolerate the food products that contain it. People with chronic degenerative conditions who do not have celiac disease may also benefit from a gluten-free diet.

A SIMPLE REMEDY: THE ELIMINATION DIET
People who suffer from chronic disease, no matter what symptoms of degenerative disease they are experiencing, can benefit

from an *elimination* diet. This is the time-honored practice used to diagnose food-related symptoms of disease and the best-known procedure for identifying food sensitivities.

By eliminating all foods except those that are the most nutritionally dense and the least likely to cause problems for highly sensitive individuals, many people discover what it is like to feel exceptionally well. I call it a clean regimen, a power regimen and a high-energy, rejuvenating regimen.

My own effective elimination diet and health and restoration regimen in the early 1990s featured:

- Essential fatty acids omega-3 and omega-6 with cold-water fish and freshly-ground flaxseed every day

- Dark-green, leafy vegetables

- Cruciferous vegetables (e.g., broccoli, radishes, cauliflower)

- Sweet potatoes (raw and cooked) and all types of squash (raw and cooked)

- Great quantities of watery vegetables (e.g., cucumbers, celery)

- No fruits for over a year, except avocados

- Intact (non-glutinous) grains—varieties of organic long- and short-grain rice.

- Spelt and kamut (both ancient forms of wheat), which were later added to my diet

I continue to eat these foods on a regular basis. To feel my best, I still limit the amount of fruit that I eat, and I do not regularly consume grains containing gluten. I eat a wide variety of nonstarchy (low-glycemic) vegetables and beans. I eat sardines or salmon—often both—daily, with large salads containing green leafy vegetables, shredded sweet potatoes and a great variety of vegetables. I enjoy intact buckwheat or quinoa, with freshly ground flaxseed and nonfat, organic soymilk. I begin and end each day with a "green drink" containing dehydrated, organic cereal grasses (e.g., barley grass, wheat grass and oat grass).

My husband and children have far more diversified regimens. The guiding principle is to find the whole foods and the balance of macronutrients (carbohydrates, protein and fats) that provide energy, stamina and freedom from disease. Eating well to feel well should be our goal.

WELCOME CONFIRMATION

In the late 1990s, I conducted a seminar in St. Augustine, Florida. Physician friends there introduced me to books and seminar notebooks by Jeffrey S. Bland, Ph.D., whose twenty-six-year career in nutritional biochemistry has spanned roles as a researcher, professor and internationally recognized expert in human nutrition. In May of 2000, my husband and I were privileged to attend a six-hour conference conducted by Jeffrey Bland.

When I discovered Dr. Bland's work, I found the research to support the foods that I had chosen as the foundation of my "elimination regimen" in the early 1990s. As I look back at the time when I was physically the weakest, baffled by health problems and concerned about my children who needed my full attention, wisdom and stamina, I am encouraged by the faithfulness of God.

Yes, I read for hours and hours. I was not computer literate at the time, and I had no worldwide web of information. Making sense out of material that was not within my academic area of expertise presented some challenges. I knew that it was clearly my responsibility to do everything that I could do to get well. I had already learned that when I came to the end of my strength and ability, God would be there. The certainty that God is with us and that we are never alone is the faith that gives us eyes that recognize and accept real solutions like those Dr. Bland offered.

HEREDITARY TENDENCIES

Dr. Bland's work has also helped me to understand the connection between my health challenges and my own hereditary tendencies. My maternal great-grandmother, Nora Edna Childers (a strong, very trim, amazingly charitable and endearing Christian woman that I remember vividly), developed Type 2 diabetes in her sixties. Three of her thirteen children, my great-uncles Howard and Web, and my grandmother, Ora, also developed Type 2 diabetes.

Another of my great-grandmother's children, my great uncle Shirley, had Type 1 diabetes. He died at age twenty-four.

Looking back over three decades since my first husband's illness in 1972, I now know that our mental, emotional and spiritual strength and maturity are works in progress. We respond to trauma, to the life-threatening illnesses of the people we love and to the deaths of the people closest to us according to the light we have on each step of the journey. As our faith becomes stronger and we are more trusting, traumatic life events no longer increase our susceptibility to disease.

Life gets richer with each decade. By seeking an optimal diet, by finally experiencing the enormous therapeutic benefits of physical conditioning and, most of all, by learning to depend on the Lord Jesus Christ in every area of my life, I have the strength and stamina at age fifty-five that I enjoyed during my best days from my teens through the following decades.

Insulin Sensitivity—a Marker for Life Span

The length of our lives, as well as the quality of life we enjoy, depends on how well our bodies handle insulin. Simply defined, insulin is a hormone that promotes the utilization of sugars, handles protein synthesis and is involved in other vital activities of the body. Type 2 diabetes, which may account for about 90 to 95 percent of all undiagnosed cases of diabetes, usually begins as insulin resistance, a disorder in which the cells do not use insulin properly.[15]

Knowing the way insulin works, recognizing our individual genetic or hereditary tendencies and being "tuned in" to our unique responses to insulin encourage us to develop dietary and lifestyle habits that will enable us to prevent and reverse chronic conditions. When we understand how the balance of macronutrients (proteins, carbohydrates and fats) affects the body, we can escape the "diet dilemma" forever. Each of us needs to know how our own body is dealing with insulin. This understanding is a basic component in overcoming any chronic degenerative disease.

I referred earlier to the ACAM (American College for the Advancement in Medicine) convention in Dallas, Texas, that I attended in May 2000. Some of the most gifted researchers and physicians in alternative medicine were presenters at that event.

93

It was exciting to be with friends and celebrate the work of health professionals who are making a difference in the lives of many people.

A day earlier, at the Anti-Aging Conference that preceded the convention, I heard Ron Rosedale's presentation, "Aging—Critical Role of Diet and Insulin." Dr. Rosedale drew a crowd because his effective protocols for treating people in acute stages of diabetes and chronic disease caught the attention of every health practitioner in the audience. He approaches treatment of disease from a molecular and cellular basis. He says, "I get down as deep as possible to find the cause in the cellular physiology, so I can appropriately deal with disease with far better results than conventional medical practice would be able to."[16]

Dr. Rosedale conducts in-depth testing of his patients, including blood, salivary, urine, insulin, heavy metals, hormone levels and electrolytes. He's looking for how everything is functioning inside the cell. His patients' first appointment lasts about four hours, which includes a one-and-one-half-hour visit with him and an hour with the nutritionist. He says that he often gets calls from conventional medical doctors who want to know what he does at the center. Dr. Rosedale confirms that his approach to treatment of disease from the molecular level is definitely an exploding field. He believes it will be the way medicine is practiced ten to twenty years from now. Comparing his medical practice as a conventional medical doctor to the way he treats patients now, he says he is more effective now because "we really get to a much deeper cause than just treating surface symptoms."[17]

Dr. Rosedale explains how we become insulin sensitive, causing us to enter into the first stages of diabetes. When the body receives more sugar than it needs, insulin is released to take the sugar and store it in the body as glycogen. Since our body stores very little glycogen, once we fill our glycogen stores, our body stores the sugar as saturated fat. All excess carbohydrates are stored in the body as saturated fat.

A surge of sugar means a surge of insulin. Too much insulin releasing has negative effects on the body. A few of these effects are retention of sodium, loss of calcium and rise of triglycerides. Insulin also accelerates the aging process.[18]

Of the estimated thirteen to fourteen million people in the United States with diabetes, between 90 and 95 percent have Type 2 diabetes (non-insulin dependent), including an increasing number of children. The typical American diet with its highly refined carbohydrates (sugar) and its abundance of refined sugar products is responsible for this preventable degenerative disease

GUIDELINES FOR REVERSING
CHRONIC DEGENERATIVE DISEASES

Dietary guidelines for people with gluten intolerance (celiacs), irritable bowel syndrome, inflammatory bowel disease and diabetes (Type 1 and Type 2) are especially helpful for the general population. They offer important strategies for preventing and reversing a wide range of degenerative disorders.

For example, most of the foods that I consume every day would be ideal for someone who has celiac sprue (gluten intolerance). If I suffered from celiac disease (a type of irritable bowel disorder), I would only need to eliminate intact spelt berries and intact wheat berries (both of which contain gluten), as well as the flour that we mill from those grains. All other foods on my regimen would promote optimal health.

I have learned to enjoy a wide variety of grains that do not contain gluten, all of which make lovely muffins, nonyeast bread and flat bread. The world is full of healthy people who regularly consume grains that do not contain gluten. They find pleasure in uncomplicated dietary regimens featuring whole foods. There is a whole world of food that does not cause the body to degenerate. When we eat a variety of whole foods, including intact grains, and fresh, organic fruits and vegetables, we get all of the micronutrients and fiber that we need. Meeting nutritional needs doesn't have to be an ordeal.

AVOIDING PROCESSED FOODS

When I look at the long, complicated lists of dos and don'ts for those who have celiac sprue, I cringe because the greatest problems that commonly plague celiacs arise when they ingest gluten *accidentally* when eating processed food. These convenience foods are high in fat, low in fiber, and they are not good choices for those who seek optimal health.

The issue that must be addressed to prevent or reverse degenerative disease is the problem of eating processed food in general. For example, a celiac can safely order in a restaurant in the same way that I do, and as many careful people do. First, request whole foods, and second, request that the foods be prepared simply. Dining out in America can certainly be safe, nutritious and delightful if we learn how to make appropriate choices in restaurants that serve real food.

Salmon, dark-green leafy salads and baked sweet potatoes are increasingly more common in restaurants. In communities across the nation, more and more restaurants feature organic food and specialize in whole-food cuisine. In our area, we have whole-food supermarkets with delis and cafeterias that serve delicious whole foods. The vegetables and grains are of excellent quality. Businesses such as these are the true "super" markets, and they are increasing in number across the country. A considerable number of consumers have come to understand that organic vegetables of good quality are particularly delicious.

People with seemingly mild cases of irritable bowel (occasional bloating, flatulence, rectal itching, indigestion and heartburn) can benefit from following the minimal dietary guidelines we discuss in this section. However, as a practical and preventative measure, individuals who walk around feeling tired most of the time should also pursue an optimal (more limited) regimen of whole foods until they feel strong and symptom-free again.

IRRITABLE BOWEL SYNDROME

Many people have recurrent symptoms throughout their lives that include intermittent pain accompanied by constipation or diarrhea (or an alternating occurrence of both). Physicians often suggest that the causes cannot be determined and that there is no "demonstrable disease."

The patient's distress, inability to function normally and physical weaknesses require the physicians to get a thorough history of the patient and follow a careful diagnostic procedure in order to rule out cancer and inflammatory bowel disease, both of which often have similar symptoms. Common diagnostic tests are *sigmoidoscopy* (examination of the colon), *barium X-ray examination* and *testing of the patient's feces.*

Gastroenterologists report that more than half the patients they see suffer from irritable bowel syndrome and that it is the most common disorder of the intestine. It is also the most common of all chronic disorders. Some experts suspect that well over 20 percent of the population suffers from irritable bowel.

People with irritable bowel suffer from an involuntary muscle movement in the large intestine in spite of the fact that they have no abnormality in the intestinal structure. Textbook descriptions of the disorder often report that those who suffer from irritable bowel disease neither gain nor lose weight. That is not necessarily true. Mainstream medical sources also state that irritable bowel syndrome does not cause sufferers to become malnourished. That is also incorrect.

Those suffering from irritable bowel syndrome complain most often about bloating and abdominal cramping. Suffering is temporarily relieved by bowel movements or by passing gas. Many people with irritable bowel syndrome never feel as though they have had a complete evacuation of the bowel. They often have mucus in the feces and discomfort, or pain, after each meal. As a result of poor digestion and assimilation, sufferers experience a wide range of symptoms secondary to bowel irritation: dizziness, nervousness, fatigue, loss of memory, anxiety, depression, palpitations, heartburn, back pain and the list goes on.

What do conventional physicians frequently prescribe? Patients who experience constipation are offered bulk-forming agents such as bran. Drugs are prescribed to relieve spasms and to treat prolonged bouts of diarrhea. The long-term effects of wheat bran, antispasmodic drugs and antidiarrheal drugs are not positive. Although physicians recommend medication and dietary fiber in order to alleviate symptoms (in the short-term), such remedies are not useful in curing irritable bowel syndrome.

DIVERTICULOSIS

Diverticulosis is a bowel syndrome in which the inner lining of the intestine, or other organs, protrudes and creates small sacs (diverticula). A wide range of symptoms and complications

97

characterize this disease. The diverticula usually affect the lower part of the colon (the main section of the large intestine). Symptoms of diverticulosis include a bloated sensation, frequent pain in the lower abdomen and alternating attacks of constipation and diarrhea. Within the remaining discussion of bowel disorders, we will outline important steps to take in order to overcome a wide range of chronic bowel afflictions. By making essential dietary and lifestyle changes and by rejoicing in the healing power of the Spirit we are able to improve, reverse and totally overcome the most severe disorders.

Twenty percent of the patients with diverticulosis are symptomatic. Many patients suffer from the same symptoms as those with irritable bowel syndrome. Many people have both conditions. Physicians need to rule out cancer if patients have symptoms of diverticulosis. Hemorrhage is rare, but possible. Most allopathic (conventional physicians) prescribe fiber supplements and antispasmodic drugs for treatment.

DIVERTICULITIS

Diverticulitis of the bowel is the result of inflammation and perforation of the diverticula. The inflammation and perforations cause pain and fever. Standard treatment includes rest and antibiotics. In severe cases, patients are fed intravenous fluids. In cases of peritonitis (inflammation of the membranous coat lining the abdominal cavity), or if perforation causes a large abscess, surgery is often necessary. When surgery is required, the diseased section is removed and the remaining sections are joined together.

Some patients require a temporary colostomy. A colostomy is a procedure that contrives an artificial anus at the body surface where it meets part of the large intestine. Obviously, the time to get alarmed is when diverticula are discovered and before diverticulosis becomes symptomatic. But if you suffer from this advanced disease, never give up hope for healing and restoration, no matter how great the degeneration. Simple regimens for optimal health can put you on the pathway to total restoration.

COLITIS AND ULCERATIVE COLITIS

Colitis is simply an inflammation of the colon. Conventional medical texts suggest that viral infections, bacterial infections such as *Campylobacter*, and even amoebas may produce toxins that irritate the lining of the colon. A course of antibiotic therapy may kill the friendly bacteria and upset the balance of power in the gastrointestinal region, thereby causing a form of colitis to occur. Not only do antibiotics kill the friendly bacteria as well as the harmful bacteria, but they also create antibiotic-resistant pathogenic bacteria.

Physicians often treat *Campylobacter* infections with erythromycin. Drugs are also used to treat amoebic infections and *Clostridium* infections. There is a better way. Drug therapies (except in emergency cases) ought never to be considered without first exploring the full range of safe and effective natural therapies. For example, lactic acid bacteria impart nutritional and therapeutic benefits to the colon that can facilitate healing naturally.

Ulcerative colitis is a chronic condition that affects between forty and fifty people per one hundred thousand. The main symptoms are bloody diarrhea and feces that contain pus and/or mucus. The inflammation and ulcers in the lining of the colon and rectum occur in the final stages of irritable bowel syndrome. The standard medical treatments to control the disease are corticosteroid drugs (which reduce the inflammation), sulfasalazine and salicylate derivatives of sulfasalazine. If the inflammation is severe and uncontrollable, the conventional medical solution is the surgical removal of the colon (colectomy). Those who suffer from the inflammation of ulcerative colitis for many years are at risk for cancer.

CROHN'S DISEASE

Crohn's disease, perhaps the most serious of the inflammatory bowel diseases, is often described as a chronic inflammation of the small bowel. However, the disease can actually affect any part of the gastrointestinal tract from the mouth to the anus. The most common site of the inflammation is at the end of the small intestine. Researchers indicate that some people are genetically predisposed to the disease.

When young people suffer from Crohn's disease, the small intestine is often the area most afflicted. The symptoms of Crohn's disease in adults and children are the same as the symptoms of other irritations of the bowel—abdominal pain and diarrhea. When Crohn's disease affects the colon, causing bloody diarrhea, it is often confused with ulcerative colitis. The most serious aspect of Crohn's disease is the increasing difficulty sufferers have in absorbing nutrients in the small intestines. The elderly experience more rectal bleeding with Crohn's. All age groups are susceptible to difficulties involving the anus such as chronic abscesses and cracks.

Nearly one-third of the people with Crohn's disease develop internal fistulas. These abnormal passages make damaging connections between internal organs and the surface of the body or between two organs. Fistulas between the intestine and the skin are common in Crohn's disease patients. Often internal fistulas develop between loops of the intestine. Abscesses develop in about 20 percent of Crohn's patients. These pockets of infection form around the anus or in the abdominal area.

Sulfasalazine and corticosteroid drugs are conventional treatments for the inflammation. Many Crohn's patients are under long-term medical supervision and experience severe attacks requiring hospital care (blood transfusions, intravenous feeding, intravenous drug therapy). As the patient degenerates, damaged parts of the small intestine need to be removed by surgery. Surgeons remove only the most affected part, anticipating degeneration to continue. Continued degeneration then necessitates further surgery. Some patients remain stable after surgery. Others do not.

Although the outlook for Crohn's is quite grim from the standpoint of conventional medicine, people are able to manage and even overcome the disease with natural therapies. The natural protocols we discuss offer every hope.

PRURITUS ANI

Pruritus is the medical term for itching, and *pruritus ani* is the term for itching of the skin around the rectum. Health professionals who are aware of the connection between *pruritus ani* and irritable bowel syndrome recognize that it is often a symptom of a digestive disorder, or of lactic acid leaking from the colon. The lactic acid causes pain, itching and bleeding.

Pruritus ani is often mistaken for hemorrhoids rather than recognized as a common symptom of any of the irritable and inflammatory bowel diseases. Often *pruritus ani* is a symptom of Crohn's disease or ulcerative colitis. Most victims of colon cancer have *pruritus ani*. This does not mean that it causes bowel cancer, but rather that it places one at risk for bowel cancer.

For immediate relief from *pruritus ani,* the sufferer needs to wash the affected area with soap and water. (Hemorrhoids are not relieved by that treatment.) However, soap and water do not eliminate the cause of the problem. *Pruritus ani* is a warning signal of something out of balance. The permanent solution is to resolve the digestive problems that cause the *pruritus.*

RESTORING HEALTH TO THE BOWELS

It is possible to restore health to your degenerating digestive system by making the right food choices and adjusting your lifestyle to eliminate harmful substances and activities. A few small steps in the right direction will reap great benefits for your quality of life.

STEP ONE: ELIMINATING HARMFUL SUGARS

Knowing just what foods, or substances, are intolerable to those with bowel disease is the first step in overcoming the symptoms of irritable bowel disease.

One of the main irritants of the bowel is sugary food, which characterizes much of the typical American diet. People with active bowel disease should avoid three sugars in particular:

- Fructose (found mainly in fruits)
- Lactose (found in dairy products)
- Alcohol sugars (sorbitol and mannitol)

Eliminating these three sugars is the important first step for those who seek to strengthen their bodies to prevent or overcome disease. Perhaps understanding why that is necessary will help to motivate sufferers to sacrifice their desire for "sweets."

FRUCTOSE. Why does fructose irritate the bowels of some people and not others? Fructose is made synthetically from corn.

It is twice as sweet as cane sugar and much cheaper. Fructose intolerance is a major cause of the most common symptoms of irritable bowel disease: cramping, diarrhea, intestinal gas and rectal itching.

Most people's metabolisms are able to convert the fructose they consume into glucose, the body's energy source. However, some people, perhaps through heredity, lack the enzyme necessary to digest fructose. For those individuals, mild to severe symptoms of irritable bowel are caused simply by eating fructose, either from whole foods (e.g., apples, oranges and bananas) or from devitalized foods containing corn syrup.

Glucose, as we mentioned, is the body's chief source of energy for each cell; it is the essential fuel that energizes the body. Even brain cells depend on glucose for their activity. The body produces glucose, a monosaccharide (simple sugar), through digestion of other carbohydrates. The cells also produce a small amount of glucose when they metabolize fats and proteins.

When we consume intact grains (grains before they are milled or flaked), this glucose fuel is released gradually into the body. This continual release of glucose energy is especially helpful as we age, because the hormones that keep the concentration of glucose within a normal range begin to work less than optimally. An optimal dietary regimen stabilizes blood sugar levels and helps restore the endocrine system, allowing us to enjoy the energy we need for quality of life.

LACTOSE. Why does lactose (milk sugar) irritate the bowels of some people and not others? Many people also lack the enzyme necessary to convert lactose to glucose. When lactose is not converted to glucose it is neither digested nor absorbed. As bacteria in the colon begin to ferment, intestinal gas, bloating, abdominal pain and diarrhea occur. The lining of the intestine becomes irritated or inflamed. A premium *Lactobacillus acidophilus* such as DDS-1 patented by the late Khem Shahani, Ph.D., a world-renowned expert in probiotics, can certainly help digest lactose.

For many people dairy is an enjoyable habit they feel good about, a food from childhood and a recreational food they do not want to eliminate. I would urge those individuals to discipline themselves to consume only certified organic dairy products. The best possible choice, in my opinion, is homemade organic soy yogurt. It is creamy, delicious and filled with live cultures and phytoestrogens.

The Physicians Committee for Responsible Medicine and Frank Oski, M.D., director of the Department of Pediatrics at Johns Hopkins University School of Medicine, recommend completely eliminating dairy products as a means of optimizing one's dietary regimen.

Many nutritionally oriented physicians have concluded that cow's milk is not suitable for human consumption. The connection between cow's milk and Type 1 diabetes is clear to many researchers, although others say the evidence is not clear at all. Many physicians also recognize that when their patients remove dairy from their dietary regimens, they are able to eliminate symptoms of asthma, congestion, arthritis, ulcerative colitis, migraine headaches and other degenerative conditions.

ALCOHOL SUGARS. As for alcohol sugars, sorbitol and mannitol, they are not digested by anyone (which, ironically, makes them calorie free). Large amounts of alcohol sugar irritate the bowels of anyone who consumes them. Sorbitol and mannitol are used as sweeteners in toothpaste, breath mints, diabetic candy and chewing gum. Manufacturers market these products as "sugar free." They are calorie free because they cannot be absorbed, but they are certainly not sugar free. Other popular products that contain sorbitol or mannitol are digestive aids, antacids, processed breakfast cereal, low-calorie syrup and chewable vitamins. Even minute amounts of these sugars can cause profound distress in sensitive individuals.

STEP TWO: DISCOVERING YOUR HEALING NUTRIENTS

The second step in completely overcoming the symptoms of irritable bowel syndrome and inflammatory bowel disease is finding sources of micronutrients that do not irritate the bowel. Those with irritable bowel are often unable to tolerate many nutrient-rich, organic whole foods. Even good foods that irritate the bowel are not good choices, no matter how rich they are in vitamins, minerals, amino acids and phytochemicals. Whole-food concentrates are often the ideal source of micronutrients in severe situations.

Those who are striving to overcome irritable bowel or inflammatory bowel disease do not want to degenerate in other areas. I recommend eating Alaskan red salmon and sardines packed in spring water three to four times a week as reliable sources of EPA and DHA, the omega-3 derivatives. Again, those who choose to consume dairy from time to time would do well to limit themselves to organic, fermented dairy. Delicious plant-based meals offer Americans real hope in making wise dietary changes.

STEP THREE: SUPPLYING NEEDED DIGESTIVE ENZYMES

The third step in becoming symptom free and in overcoming, or managing, irritable bowel disease is to supplement every healthy meal with digestive enzymes and lactic acid bacteria, as we have mentioned. Replenishing our bodies' digestive enzymes is essential for those who have spent most of their lives consuming cooked and processed foods that are totally devoid of all enzymes.

Each year more and more people find that they cannot tolerate a number of foods, many of which are nutritionally dense, whole foods. Difficulties with digestion and assimilation are widespread. Many people suffer gastrointestinal distress without seeking more than an over-the-counter remedy that offers symptomatic relief.

All of us (not just those who suffer from allergies, food intolerances, fatigue, gastrointestinal disorders and other degenerative diseases) need to completely digest the foods we eat and fully assimilate the nutrients that those foods offer. Nutritionally dense foods heal our bodies and enable us to overcome debilitating diseases, provided we have the enzymes necessary for complete digestion. However, even healing foods such as beans, intact grains, raw vegetables and freshly ground flaxseed will not heal our bodies unless we are able to digest and assimilate them.

If our bodies have not produced sufficient digestive enzymes, we need to take them in supplemental form. We also need to consume fermented foods (soy or organic dairy, yogurt, sauerkraut, tempeh and so forth) to nurture and restore the friendly microorganisms in the intestines. Without proper balance in the intestinal flora, we cannot achieve optimal health.

Look for premium digestive enzyme formulas containing

amylase, invertase, glucoamylase, protease, malt diastase, cellu-lase, peptidase, lipase, lactase and acid-stable protease. Beet root, manganese and zinc are also helpful. A supplement that provides a complete digestive complex is life changing for those with irri-table bowel syndrome.

In addition to the three steps we have discussed, individuals who are suffering from irritable bowel syndrome, even though they follow an optimal regimen, should consider having tests to determine whether or not they suffer from celiac sprue (gluten intolerance). Many people with colitis, Crohn's disease and other diseases of the bowel also suffer from gluten intolerance.

SPECIAL CONSIDERATIONS FOR CROHN'S DISEASE

Most people with Crohn's disease improve when fructose, lac-tose and the alcohol sugars are eliminated from their diets. Those who have not improved after eliminating these sugars should try to establish the following protocol.

First, eliminate the foods and substances that are known to irri-tate the bowel. Then begin to consume organic whole foods (with no processed or devitalized foods whatsoever) and supplement the diet with whole-food concentrates. If new whole foods, particularly grains, are introduced one at a time, specific intolerances can be identified. Offending foods ought to be reintroduced into the diet from time to time as the sufferer gains strength.

Whole foods that must be eliminated are all of the fructose-containing fruits (apples, bananas, cherries, grapes, melons, peaches, pears, pineapples, and so forth). The fruits that do not irri-tate the bowel are tomatoes and avocados. Honey and corn sweet-eners, and all products containing them, are especially offensive. By eliminating all processed foods and recreational food-like products (carbonated beverages and candy, for example), the focus changes from disease maintenance to restoration of optimal health.

Those people suffering with severe irritable bowel disease should not mourn the fact that they cannot use convenience foods or order from a restaurant menu indiscriminately. The healthiest people in the world do not pull their foods off the shelves of supermarkets, processed, devitalized and loaded with fat and high-fructose corn sweeteners.

Those who are struggling with this disease may look forward to overcoming food intolerances, as well as the debilitating effects of Crohn's disease itself. An extremely important healing protocol that is essential in managing Crohn's disease optimally is to consume digestive enzymes and friendly bacteria of fermented foods (probiotic formulations).

PROBIOTICS—KEY TO THE SECOND IMMUNE SYSTEM

The vital role of fermented food and lactic acid bacteria has never been taught to most modern Americans. For centuries, people in much of the world have preserved food with lactic acid bacteria. Without proper refrigeration, it was necessary to use fermentation processes to preserve foods. Milk became yogurt. Cabbage was preserved as sauerkraut. Eggs were pickled, and meats were preserved through fermenting processes as well.

On a medical mission trip to Ukraine, I was delighted to discover the great number of fermented foods that the Eastern Europeans consume throughout the year. I also realized why they are able to remain free of bacterial infections in spite of the less than sanitary methods in which meat and dairy products are handled in the open-air markets.

Nearly every vegetable they grow in the summer is preserved by fermentation for consumption in the fall, winter and spring. These strong, hardy people flourish under hardship and deprivation. None of the Ukrainians I met had ever considered the great health benefit in preserving food through fermentation—they fermented food simply for sake of survival during the winter. Such survival skills have been passed down to them for centuries.

Modern industrialized societies, such as ours, are quick to discard the old ways in favor of convenience. Fermented foods would still be consumed in every household if we understood the value of the microorganisms they supply and purposed to acquire a taste for these extraordinarily beneficial foods. Their value to our health has long been recognized:

> Metchnikoff [Eli Metchnikoff, *The Prolongation of Life*] was perhaps the first researcher, and he concluded in 1908 that the long life span of the Balkans was due to the ingestion of large quantities of lactobacilli and

other lactic organisms through fermented foods, which inhibit pathogens and detoxify their systems.[19]

OUR SPECIAL NEED FOR FRIENDLY BACTERIA

In our twenty-first century culture, we need the healing power of fermented foods and lactobacilli (friendly bacteria) more than ever. Most people have ingested antibiotics or consumed meat, poultry or dairy that has been injected with antibiotics. Antibiotics have destroyed the beneficial bacteria in the intestines along with the harmful bacteria. Drugs, processed foods, stress, environmental toxins and impure water can also alter the balance between friendly and harmful bacteria. We must reestablish the friendly bacteria in order to protect ourselves from both infectious and degenerative disease. Scientific research concurs:

> Our intestines harbor hundreds of species of bacteria, both beneficial and harmful. Probiotics are the microorganisms which may prevent or reduce the effect of an infection caused by a pathogenic organism...Lactic acid producing bacteria have the ability to kill pathogenic bacteria by secreting small quantities of antibiotic-like substances including lactic acid, acetic acid, benzoic acid, hydrogen peroxide, etc. Probiotics are thought to confer a "second immune system" to the host by virtue of their role in preventing pathogens, also by producing B vitamins, improving natural gastrointestinal balance and stimulating immune response.[20]

Irritable bowel syndrome predisposes sufferers to cancer. Again, with appropriate dietary protocols, supplementation with whole food concentrates and use of digestive enzymes and friendly bacteria, the degenerative process can be reversed.

These protocols for overcoming irritable bowel syndrome are useful for anyone seeking to achieve optimal health. Those who are in great pain or experiencing profound inflammation will need to endure a very restrictive diet for a time. But the encouraging news is that dietary changes can enable sufferers to overcome the debilitating symptoms of irritable bowel syndrome and inflammatory bowel disease.

How to Begin Whole-Food Therapy

Many people who are suffering from irritable bowel simply cannot begin with high-fiber foods. They are too ill to digest these foods properly. I recommend they begin with certified organic whole food concentrates; these are vegetable and fruit juices from which the fiber has been removed. When the juice is extracted from organic raw foods, the micronutrients are immediately available to feed the body at the cellular level. All of the enzymes that are necessary to digest the food are available in the food when it is in its raw state.

Those who suffer from irritable bowel disease and inflammatory bowel disease must often eliminate raw vegetables from their regimen until healing and restoration occur in the region of the gut. However, they can readily assimilate the healing powers of these foods in their juiced state, when the fiber has been removed.

Dehydrated juice from young cereal grasses (green juice) may provide the widest spectrums of naturally occurring nutrients available in a single source. Look for products that do not contain binders, fillers, artificial colors or preservatives. The natural chlorophyll in the young cereal grasses heal the irritated and inflamed bowel.

Organic white rice and organic flaxseed oil are also important for healing the bowel. They supply the macronutrients (protein, carbohydrates and fats). They are also well tolerated by those in acute stages of irritable bowel disease. Even though the fiber and outer layer of the rice (containing many of the nutrients) have been removed, the grain still contains protein, carbohydrates and some nutrients.

Often we must begin eating very simply in order to overcome degenerative disease. Each person must become aware of the healing process and appreciate improvements in his or her own body. If we are determined to do what we can in order to walk in wellness, we are more likely to recognize the great significance of even small changes.

Protocols for Treating Type 1 and Type 2 Diabetes

The protocols for the prevention and cure of Type 2 diabetes include those health regimens we have discussed for the prevention and cure of chronic degenerative disease. Eliminating the problematic sugars and following the healthy regimen outlined earlier for restoring health can be effective in reversing the onset of Type 2 diabetes.

Diabetics are at greater risk for atherosclerosis (narrowing of the arteries), hypertension (high blood pressure) and other diseases involving the cardiovascular system. Thus the regimen that best allows the insulin-dependent (Type 1) diabetic to control the disease, and that clearly enables the non-insulin-dependent diabetic (Type 2) to reverse the disease, also helps to prevent Type 2 diabetes and other degenerative diseases as well.

Type 1 diabetes

Type 1 diabetes, previously called insulin-dependent diabetes mellitus (IDDM) or juvenile-onset diabetes, only accounts for 5 to 10 percent of all diagnosed cases of diabetes. Risk factors for Type 1 diabetes include autoimmune, genetic and environmental factors. When the body's immune system destroys pancreatic beta cells, Type 1 diabetes develops. Pancreatic beta cells are the only cells in the body that make the hormone insulin, which is absolutely necessary to regulate blood glucose.

When the cells that secrete insulin are destroyed, the body simply stops producing insulin. Without insulin, sugar cannot get to the cells where it is needed. Regular injections of insulin are necessary in order to prevent the diabetic from going into a coma and dying as a consequence.

Type 1 diabetes progresses rapidly and usually manifests itself in people under age thirty-five. It commonly develops in children ten to sixteen years of age. Researchers think that Type 1 diabetes develops as an immune response to a viral infection. This response may be delayed, resulting years after the damage to the pancreas occurs. Diagnoses of Type 1 diabetes have been recorded as having risen sharply after viral epidemics.

Mumps and German measles are common viruses associated with diabetes. It is important to recognize that the viruses are not the direct cause of diabetes. Rather, it is widely believed that the immune system mistakes the insulin-secreting cells in the pancreas (beta cells) for the proteins contained in the viruses. The immune system then destroys the beta cells in the pancreas that are so very similar to the virus particles. When the beta cells are destroyed, the body cannot produce insulin. There are also drugs and chemicals that destroy the body's ability to produce insulin. Two prescription drugs can trigger insulin-dependent diabetes: pentamidine (used to treat pneumonia) and L-asparaginase (a cancer treatment).[21] According to articles in the *New England Journal of Medicine* (1992) and the *American Journal of Clinical Nutrition* (1990), another possible cause of Type 1 diabetes is the consumption of cow's milk. This is, of course, controversial.

Studies indicate that the immune systems of a great number of children cannot differentiate between the cow's milk protein particles and the pancreatic islet cells. Thus, in reacting to the cow's milk, the body destroys the insulin-producing cells as well. Studies showing that high levels of antibodies to the cow's milk protein particles have been found in newly diagnosed diabetics strengthen this theory. There is enough evidence to give consumers pause.

Parents who are convinced their children need cow's milk to supplement the calcium ought to consider other sources for calcium intake. Certainly, one way to be sure that our supply of calcium is adequate is to avoid calcium-depleting animal proteins—the high phosphorus content of animal products drives calcium out of the body. Another solution is to consume calcium-rich foods such as kale, green leafy vegetables, beans and tofu. These foods are not only rich in vitamins, minerals and amino acids, but they are also filled with life-saving phytochemicals as well.

TYPE 2 DIABETES

Type 2 diabetes is another matter. The body still produces insulin, but it has become resistant to proper utilization of the insulin. Obesity is often a key factor in developing Type 2 diabetes. Type 2 diabetes is considered a chronic illness without a cure, but is it? Although those who develop Type 2 diabetes cannot overcome their symptoms without making significant dietary and lifestyle changes, appropriate changes do enable sufferers to overcome their illness.

Many people suffer from glucose intolerance, an abnormal

response to large amounts of sugar. Others suffer, to some degree, from even small amounts of simple sugar. For those individuals, even fruit—in spite of the fact that it contains fiber—causes the blood sugar to rise too rapidly. Symptoms of that reaction to sugar range from headache and fatigue to wet palms and dizziness. As the blood sugar rises rapidly, it causes a sharp insulin response and then precipitates a hypoglycemic reaction. Dietary and lifestyle changes can break this cycle and restore health and well-being.

SPECIAL CONSIDERATIONS FOR DIABETICS

For those suffering with any form of diabetes, their goal should be to get lean and strong by following an optimal dietary regimen (consuming the best fats, unrefined carbohydrates and plant proteins) and by establishing an optimal fitness regimen (aerobic exercise, stretching and strength training). Achieving optimal weight, however, is only one aspect of walking in wellness.

THE "FAT" OFFENDER

One of the greatest offenders in the diet of the diabetic is fat intake:

> Fat is a problem for diabetics. The more fat there is in the diet, the harder time insulin has in getting sugar into the cell...Modern diabetic treatment programs drastically reduce meats, high-fat dairy products, and oils. At the same time, they increase grains, legumes, and vegetables.[22]

Having said that fat is problematic, however, one cannot conclude that a diet without fat will restore health to the diabetic or to anyone for that matter. It is the right kinds of fats that produce optimal health.

ESSENTIAL FATTY ACIDS

All of the billions of cells in the body need essential fatty acids found in fats and oils. Essential fatty acids (EFAs) are truly *essential* for the body. They enable nutrients to enter the cells. They also maintain the cell membranes, which are actually liquid barriers surrounding the cells. EFAs regulate the immune system, the cardiovascular system, the digestive system and the reproductive system. And they play an essential role in controlling the metabolic rate, the neural circuits in the brain, the healing and repair process and inflammation. These hormone-like chemicals regulate cellular activity on a moment-by-moment basis, actually enabling our bodies to burn calories.

Fatty acids must be ingested from our diet because the body cannot produce them. Diabetes is only one of the degenerative conditions that may develop as a result of a fatty acid deficiency. Without the essential fatty acids, we increase our risk of heart disease, cancer and stroke. We need to limit our fat intake to the essential and beneficial fats; then we will not crave the inferior or harmful fats.

There are two families of essential fatty acids. One is the omega-3 family; the other is the omega-6 family. Alpha-linolenic acid belongs to the omega-3 family and is found in dark-green leafy vegetables and organic flaxseed. Flaxseed can be ground in seconds by using a small, inexpensive coffee grinder. This is important because it assures freshness; oils that become rancid are harmful to the body. The whole flaxseed is also valuable because it contains lignans that are high in phytoestrogens (plant estrogens). Research indicates that the lignans from flaxseed, like the isoflavones in soy, "are converted to biologically active hormone-like substances by intestinal microflora" and "may be cancer protective agents."[23]

Omega-3 EFAs are also found in cold-water fish such as salmon, sardines, mackerel or herring. The Center for Science in the Public Interest reports that salmon is the fish that is most free from contaminants. Many fatty acid researchers consider Alaskan red salmon in particular to be the cold-water fish that is most free of pollutants and thus the safest to eat.

Dr. Walter Willett, M.D. presented astounding research findings supporting the enormous benefit—from a cardiovascular standpoint—that we derive from eating cold-water fish:

> In randomized trials among individuals with existing coronary disease, high intake of fish or omega-3 fatty acid supplements has resulted in a reduction of coro-

nary heart disease recurrence specifically due to a substantial decrease in sudden death. Thus the evidence that higher intake of omega-3 fatty acids can reduce coronary heart disease mortality due to sudden death is conclusive.[24]

Omega-6 EFAs are found primarily in raw nuts, seeds and legumes and in unsaturated vegetable oils, such as borage oil, grape seed oil and soybean oil. One of the richest sources of omega-6 fatty acid is the soybean. Whole organic soybeans are very different from the wide range of highly processed food products made from soybeans. I recommend organic whole soybeans and organic tofu, or bean curd, a highly concentrated soybean product. Again, research indicates that isoflavones in soybeans may be powerful cancer-protective agents. The high intake of soybeans, according to research, may account for the low mortality in breast and prostate cancer of Japanese women and men, respectively.[25]

MONOUNSATURATED FAT

Monounsaturated fatty acids found in rich, extra-virgin olive oil are another important type of fat the body needs for optimal health. It is important not to squander our allotment of fat grams on meat, poultry, dairy and fish (other than an appropriate amount of cold-water fish), because we need to spend those fat grams on the fats that truly build health.

In connection with a diet rich in unrefined, high-fiber plant foods, low in saturated fats and high in essential fatty acids, the diabetic, like everyone else seeking to overcome degenerative disease, can profit from consuming extra-virgin olive oil.

As we have discussed, the Mediterranean culture of the 1960s was one of the healthiest on earth. What kind of olive oil did they consume in that region in the 1960s? They enjoyed extra-virgin quality, made from a simple, traditional process. Producers made the oil without heat, and it still contained all of the natural qualities unique to olives. (Heating olive oil not only causes it to lose its value; it makes it become mutation-causing as well. Extra-virgin olive oil has not been de-gummed, refined, bleached or deodorized. If the olive oil is not labeled "extra-virgin," then it is refined.

Besides these important dietary considerations to help you

113

along your pathway to total health and restoration, there are also lifestyle issues that will determine your quality of life.

THE FAITH PARADIGM

Throughout our discussion of ways to establish optimal health, I want to remind you that the mind, will and emotions can, and often do, override both the best and worst dietary and lifestyle habits. To say it another way, in spite of the worst dietary and lifestyle habits, faith and trust provide resilience in the face of life's highs and lows, tragedies and joyful events.

In fact, it would be impossible to overstate the benefits of spiritual well-being. Walking in love, joy and peace as well as mercy and forgiveness boost the immune system and enable us to walk in physical health. Conversely, it is possible to follow an optimal dietary lifestyle regimen and still find trouble mentally, emotionally and physically if we lack spiritual vitality.

The most important part of a journey to health and healing is to learn how to escape fear, anger and bitterness and other negative responses to life that wreak havoc with our health—mind, soul and body. As we learn to walk by God's grace in forgiveness of those who injure us and to possess a faith that allows us to find peace in the deepest and darkest losses life brings to us, we will ensure our journey to optimal health.

We can—through activities that strengthen the body, mind and spirit—rest in the certainty that each of us is able to overcome our genetic predispositions, alter our biochemistry and become physically, mentally and emotionally more resilient

We can expect our loving God, who desires for us to enjoy health, to enable us with His divine power to do what we need to do on our journey to health. My prayer for you can be expressed in the apostle Paul's words to all believers:

> I pray that you will begin to understand the incredible greatness of his power for us who believe him. This is the same mighty power that raised Christ from the dead and seated him in the place of honor at God's right hand in the heavenly realms.
>
> **—EPHESIANS 1:19–20**

How We Heal

Balancing Your Hormones

KEY QUESTIONS

1. **W**HAT IS ESTROGEN DOMINANCE? **W**HAT SYMPTOMS OF ESTROGEN DOMINANCE DO MANY WOMEN EXPERIENCE? **M**EN? **C**HILDREN?

2. **W**HY DO MOST CONVENTIONAL BIOMEDICAL PHYSICIANS PRESCRIBE ESTROGENS AND PROGESTERONE THAT ARE NOT BIOIDENTICAL HORMONES (I.E., HORMONES WITH THE SAME MOLECULAR STRUCTURE AS THE HORMONES MADE BY THE HUMAN BODY)?

3. **W**HY ARE HAZARDOUS HORMONES MANUFACTURED, SOLD AND PROMOTED WHEN SAFE, AND EVEN MORE EFFECTIVE, BIOIDENTICAL HORMONES ARE AVAILABLE?

As we have mentioned, health is a continuum; that is to say, optimal health cannot be separated into "parts" but must be considered as a continuous whole. Perhaps eliminating some harmful foods or activities will help you progress in your journey to total health and restoration. However, if you fail to consider the continuum of health, the whole gamut of issues that promote and ensure optimal health, you may be disappointed in the outcome of the measures you have implemented to restore health.

I encourage you to continue your journey by gaining needed understanding regarding the function of hormonal balance as it contributes to your health. Those men, women and children who suffer either the distress of menopausal symptoms, premenstrual syndrome or symptoms of andropause (male menopause) need to be alerted to the fact that their bodies are out of balance and in a degenerative state.

If we don't examine the hormonal issues involved in PMS, or if we laughingly dismiss hot flashes as "power surges," we trivialize serious health issues. Hot flashes and night sweats are positive only if we view them as warning signals that demand action. These symptoms indicate that our bodies are out of balance and consequently, running low on strength and power.

The discomforts of PMS and the distress that women feel during perimenopause, menopause and postmenopause simply tell us, among other things, that our current dietary and lifestyle regimens are not solving our problems. If we understand the connection between dietary and lifestyle habits and hormonal imbalance, we have taken the first giant leap to begin to solve our health-related problems. Apart from the dietary and lifestyle choices that make Americans world leaders in obesity and degenerative disease, we face enormous challenges as a result of environmental pollution. The role of petrochemical derivatives in the problem of estrogen dominance, a condition that causes great distress for millions, is undeniable.

What Is Estrogen Dominance?

When the estrogen in the body is not in proper balance with progesterone, when estrogen levels are higher than is desirable, it is accurate to say that estrogen becomes the dominant hormone. To understand why this is a major problem, we need to understand the physiological effects of both estrogen and progesterone.

Progesterone and estrogen are made in the adrenal glands. Progesterone is also made in the testes of the male. The ovaries of menstruating women also produce progesterone and estrogen. Progesterone is made just prior to ovulation, and its levels increase rapidly after ovulation to become the major female gonadal (sex gland) hormone during the latter two weeks of the menstrual cycle.

During the last several decades, the biomedical system and the pharmaceutical industry have grappled with their knowledge of and treatment for hormonal imbalance and the serious threat it is to our health. Controversy has raged around such life-threatening issues as osteoporosis, uterine cancer and breast cancer. Serious issues also surround the fertility of younger women as well as the sperm levels of young men.

Answers from the biomedical establishment to these health issues are insufficient. Yet, once again they have tried to silence other voices of dedicated researchers and physicians who are addressing these health issues with natural protocols that have produced remarkable results.

ERT AND HRT

The following well-financed biomedical-pharmaceutical-industrial point of view dominates the media, the market and the medical schools. The estrogen replacement therapy (ERT) and hormone replacement therapy (HRT) they recommend do not involve the use of bioidentical hormones with the same molecular structure as the hormones our bodies produce. They are pushing the deadly progestins, synthetic estrogen and horse estrogen. (Premarin is made from the urine of pregnant mares.)

Their four main statements fail to address the real issues women face, and they fail to point to safe and effective solutions. They are common assertions used to market synthetic estrogens and progestins (synthetic progesterone) that have dangerous side effects—as clearly described on their package inserts.

THE SPIN USED TO MARKET ESTROGEN

1. The midlife female body gradually produces an insufficient amount of estrogen, as cycles become longer and scant.

2. Menopausal women need estrogen treatment to prevent osteoporosis and heart disease.

3. The risk of endometrial cancer as a result of estrogen replacement therapy or hormone replacement therapy (estrogen plus progestin or progesterone) is small compared to the disease risk as a result of not taking estrogen.

4. The risk of heart disease as a result of an estrogen deficiency at menopause and during the post-menopausal period is great.

INAPPROPRIATE THERAPIES

Drug manufacturers change the molecular structure of progesterone and the estrogens in order to develop products that can be patented. In doing so, they *alter* miraculous, life-extending, life-saving bioidentical hormones (hormones with exactly the same molecular structure as the hormones produced by the human body) and turn them into dangerous drugs. These patented hormones create enormous profits for the pharmaceutical industry; however, research clearly indicates that altering the natural hormonal structures poses health risks and are life-threatening for those who take them. Apart from all of the research studies, physicians and their patients have only to read the package inserts for the warnings they contain. There are many choices to make in overcoming hormonal imbalance, but the truth is this: Conventional estrogen replacement therapy (ERT) and conventional hormone replacement therapy (HRT) are unthinkable options for those who understand and acknowledge the full range of safe and effective options that are available.

Unopposed estrogen

Studies from the 1970s revealed that when estrogen is given alone (known as unopposed estrogen), without a progestin or progesterone, it carries with it a high risk of endometrial cancer and possibly other cancers, including breast cancer. Through a landmark journal article published in 1975 the news got out that women on estrogen replacement therapy (ERT) had a 7.6 times greater risk of cancer.[26] Patients who have been advised by their physicians to take unopposed estrogen (and amazingly enough, many women continue to be ill advised) need to get a copy of this journal article. I suggest they give a copy to their physician and ask whether she/he knew about the research, and if so, what she/he has in mind.

Premarin was the most commonly prescribed estrogen at that time, just as it is now. Over six million women were using Premarin in 1975. We do not know how many women died as a result of the high dosages of Premarin used in the 1960s and 1970s; we simply know that many did. The protocols advocated by many doctors contributed to the spread of misinformation that led to the deaths of an indeterminable number of women.

When medical journals began to publish their findings that showed increased risk of uterine cancer among women who took synthetic estrogen, what was the response? What did the pharmaceutical industry and the medical community do when the dangers of unopposed estrogen were exposed? Concerned physicians report:

> The dosages of Premarin were lowered, and based on studies showing that the addition of a progestin decreased the likelihood of uterine cancer in women, those women with an intact uterus were given Provera with the Premarin. Women without a uterus, it was decided, didn't need the "protective" properties of progesterone, as lacking a uterus eliminated the risk of endometrial cancer. Which, of course, is true, but what about other cancers? And the necessary balancing effect of progesterone on estrogen? What about the other possible risks of unopposed estrogen?[27]

PROBLEM OF POPULAR SYNTHETIC HORMONES

The most common synthetic hormones prescribed by bio-medical doctors pose many health risks that can be avoided by choosing more effective treatments. The word *estrogen* is actually misleading. Estrogen is a generic word that refers to a class of hormones with estrous activity.

The three most important hormones in the estrogen class are estrone (E1), estradiol (E2) and estriol (E3). When estrogen is dominant, it can cause breast stimulation resulting in breast fibro-cysts and/or cancer. Premarin, which contains a combination of these three estrogens, is one of the most widely prescribed drugs in America and perhaps the most tragic in terms of the number of women who have been persuaded by their physicians to consume it.

Premarin contains horse estrogen extracted from the urine of pregnant mares. It contains 48 percent estrone, according to some sources, and up to 75 or 80 percent according to others. In either case, the percentage of estrone is too high. In the healthy human body, estrone is in balance with estradiol and estriol. That is the first problem.

The second problem is that estradiol is the circulating estrogen that increases the risk of cancer, and estrone converts to estradiol in the body, dangerously increasing those harmful levels. The natural, healthy pattern for circulating estrogens in the body is quite different from Premarin. The pattern for naturally circulating estrogens is:

- 10 to 20 percent estrone
- 10 to 20 percent estradiol
- 60 to 80 percent estriol

The third problem is that Premarin also contains equilin and equilenin (which are horse estrogens), as well as synthetic additives. These estrogens are unnatural and potentially cancer producing. Finally, any synthetic additives pose an additional health risk. Reports such as the following are very disturbing:

> Recent media attention focused on reports of an increased risk of breast cancer in women in the Nurses

Health Study who had been on estrogen longer than 5 years. What was never addressed by any of the physicians or health writers commenting on this disturbing information is that the overwhelming majority of women in the series were taking the conjugated equine estrogens, not 17-beta estradiol.[28]

PERPETUATING THE PROBLEM

Premarin has been among the most frequently prescribed drugs for over two decades. Despite all the deaths and all the dangers, physicians continue to prescribe a variety of hormones that are patented and marketed aggressively by the pharmaceutical industry.

How can this deception regarding conventional hormone replacement therapy continue? The answer is power, money and the biomedical-pharmaceutical-industrial-governmental alliance. We have to believe we can do something to change this system.

When I talk to women who are afraid to continue ERT and HRT, I find that most of them never wanted to read the package insert before they began taking the medication because they believed it would make them even more fearful. Yet, they took the drugs in spite of their fears, because a physician advised it.

Still, they find it hard to believe that there are safe and effective natural hormone therapies that offer solutions without creating problems. Why? They believe that their physician would surely know what is available and would recommend the very best products available. Dr. Lee offers this observation:

> If natural progesterone is so wonderful, why isn't it used by my doctor? This is the question that I am most frequently asked. My answer is that it is not favored by the medical-industrial complex.[29]

SILENCING CRITICAL VOICES OF MEDICAL PEERS

Dr. Prior is an associate professor of medicine, Division of Endocrinology at the University of British Columbia in Vancouver, Canada. She was invited to write a short chapter about osteoporosis to be included in a monograph for family doctors on menopause treatment. When she asked the editor (a young academic gynecologist) for guidelines, she soon realized that her real assignment was to write that all menopausal women need estrogen treatment. Since that was not her view, she candidly expressed her thoughts and discussed why her information would be helpful for doctors and the patients they served.[30]

Dr. Prior's view as a noteworthy endocrinologist does not support the biomedical system's view that depicts perimenopausal or menopausal women who suffer from hormonal imbalance as being estrogen deficient and in need of conjugated estrogen for life. For those of us who do eventually require supplemental estrogen, we need natural, safe bioidentical estrogen, as we will discuss.

What had Dr. Prior's personal experiences taught her? She understood exactly what millions of other women know about their own perimenopausal experiences:

- Symptoms of perimenopause are more like adolescence, with its hormonal imbalances, than postmenopausal symptoms.

- Just as in journeys through adolescence, the woman in midlife may encounter a variety of symptoms resulting from hormonal imbalance.

Is hormonal imbalance always caused from estrogen deficiency as conventional medicine insists? Like many perimenopausal women, Dr. Prior had hot flashes and night sweats without missing one period. Her cycles were normal or short in interval and heavy in flow. And her cycles had a normal luteal phase length of ten or more days, all of which indicate the abundant presence of estrogen. Dr. Prior's response was:

> What if I had told this editor that I believe I am currently experiencing estrogen excess! Otherwise, I find it hard to explain my short follicular phases, early and increased cervical mucus production, short cycles, breast enlargement, and nipple tenderness.[31]

In Dr. Prior's article, she cites numerous other researchers who have reached the same conclusions. She asks the most significant question:

> How is it that breast tenderness, weight gain, bloating, and mood-changes all signal high estrogen levels, when

experienced by adolescent females; and yet when the same symptoms are experienced by females during mid-life, they are read as symptoms of estrogen deficiency?[32]

The sobering truth that leaps from the pages of this journal article is that the arrogance and ignorance that silenced Jerilynn Prior run rampant in the medical profession.

Dr. Prior's story underscores the magnitude of the resistance to change: Her suggestions for the minimal improvements in standard protocols would not be tolerated. Dr. Prior's recommendation to her colleagues was of course a far safer protocol than the protocols in standard practice.

She simply recommended an increase in the dosage of synthetic progesterone (medroxyprogesterone) and a lower dose of conjugated estrogen. She advised that patients should not take the conjugated estrogen on a continuous schedule, but rather, they should take it on a cyclic schedule (0.3 mg for twenty-five days each month). [Note: Even though Dr. Prior was pleading for a much safer course of therapy, the dangers of Premarin and Provera and the hazards of progestins are now well established, as are the safety and efficacy of bioidentical hormones.]

Although this 1994 article by Jerilynn Prior, M.D., does not contain important answers, she is asking all the right questions! I do not offer Dr. Prior's article as an explanation of, or answer to, estrogen dominance. I find this article so very compelling because it typifies the plight of an inquiring and conscientious physician. This story is significant because Dr. Prior is a skillful physician. If she cannot be heard, then what will it take to overcome those who stand against irresponsible medicine?

It will take educated consumers who know what constitutes appropriate healthcare and who will demand that their physicians practice responsible medicine. Responsible physicians and consumer advocacy groups alert the public to the benefits and availability of natural progesterone.

SAFE, NATURAL ALTERNATIVES AVAILABLE

While misinformation dominated the media for decades, now many more physicians are speaking out and seeking the education they did not get in medical school (and cannot get from the pharmaceutical representatives). Many physicians do want to know how to prevent and cure degenerative disease and are disheartened, after acquiring an expensive medical education, to discover that they have not even begun a meaningful inquiry.

John R. Lee, M.D. is a pioneer, crusader and educator whose message about the role of progesterone and the importance of bioidentical hormone therapy has helped save and transform millions of lives. Dr. Lee won a scholarship to Harvard, was in the top third of his class every year and graduated with honors. He is a graduate of the University of Minnesota Medical School. Dr. Lee has devoted years to the study of optimal health and the prevention of degenerative disease.

After being "a regular doctor" for ten years, he learned that his training didn't help people to stay well. It can now be said that many physicians have been greatly influenced and have changed the way they practice medicine as a result of the work of John R. Lee. In 1978, twenty-three years after graduating from medical school and in his twentieth year of family practice, Dr. Lee heard a lecture on natural progesterone by Ray Peat, Ph.D. of Oregon. Since that time, he has devoted years to the study of optimal health and the prevention of degenerative disease.

When important information about estrogen came to light in the seventies, John R. Lee stopped in his tracks. He decided to begin practicing medicine differently. For example, Dr. Lee began experimenting using natural progesterone with patients for whom estrogen was contraindicated. He learned many things from his patients with osteoporosis. The following clinical results for treatment of osteoporosis marked the turning point in John R. Lee's life and medical practice. He came to understand that:

1. Patients not on hormones experienced 1 percent bone loss per year and 4 percent loss in three years.

2. Patients on estrogen experienced no change in bone density.

3. Patients on progesterone experienced 15 percent increase in bone density in three years!

Dr. Lee's years of treating women naturally have proven that progesterone is absolutely safe. When patients use progesterone, bone building occurs with or without estrogen. Dr. Lee says that this phenomenon should have started a revolution. Then, in good humor he adds, "I'm getting a little tired of the revolution."[33]

Dr. Lee recommends that any diagnostic or treatment program for osteoporosis begin with a bone mineral density (BMD) measurement. The patient and the physician need a baseline with which to evaluate the results of the treatment. He suggests that all women measure their height when they are thirty and continue to measure their height yearly. When the spinal bone deterioration causes a loss in height, it usually indicates osteoporosis. As Dr. Lee discusses in his books, osteoporosis is a multifactorial disease. Progesterone without proper diet, nutrients and exercise is not a proper protocol for the prevention or reversal of osteoporosis.[34]

John R. Lee offers us two especially useful lists that put the problem of estrogen dominance in perspective. The following lists make it easier to understand how to determine what bioidentical hormones we need to achieve hormonal balance. The first list describes the effects of both estrogen and progesterone. The second list names the symptoms caused or worsened by estrogen dominance.[35]

EFFECTS OF ESTROGEN AND PROGESTERONE

ESTROGEN EFFECTS	PROGESTERONE EFFECTS
Increases body fat	Protects against fibrocystic breasts
Causes breast stimulation	Helps use fat for energy
Causes salt and fluid retention	A natural antidepressant
Interferes with thyroid hormone	Facilitates thyroid hormone action
Increases blood clotting	Normalizes blood clotting
Decreases sex drive	Restores sex drive

Impairs blood sugar control	Normalizes blood sugar levels
Causes a loss of zinc and a retention of copper	Normalizes zinc and copper levels

SYMPTOMS CAUSED OR WORSENED BY ESTROGEN DOMINANCE

Aging (an acceleration of the process)

Autoimmune disorders (e.g., lupus erythematosus, thyroiditis, Sjögren's disease)

Fat around the abdomen, hips and thighs

Premenopausal bone loss

Thyroid dysfunction mimicking hypothyroidism

Premenstrual syndrome

Water retention, bloating

Allergies	Brain fog
Breast tenderness	Blood clotting (increased)
Depression	Fatigue
Fibrocystic breasts	Gallbladder disease
Headaches	Hypoglycemia
Infertility	Irritability
Loss of libido	Memory loss
Miscarriage	Osteoporosis
Uterine cancer	Uterine fibroids

Research has shown that bone loss occurs before the loss of estrogen. Our bone density peaks at age thirty-five and begins to decline sharply at age fifty-five. What causes bone loss at age thirty-five? The answer most often is low levels of progesterone. The question is, Why are women experiencing progesterone deficiencies well before midlife?

The adrenal cortex (when functioning optimally) maintains our supply of estrogen and progesterone after the ovaries no longer perform that function. Estrogen is also stored in body fat and then metabolized by the liver. Progesterone should remain in adequate supply as well. A progesterone deficiency is not "normal," but it is common. The Lord did not design our bodies to run out of progesterone or estrogen during midlife. However, in the Western industrialized world an alarming number of women are deficient in progesterone.

Research has also revealed the common causes of estrogen dominance in Western industrialized countries:

1. Estrogen replacement therapy

2. Birth control pills that have an excessive estrogen component

3. Hysterectomy (can induce subsequent ovary dysfunction or atrophy)

4. Obesity during the menopausal and post-menopausal periods

5. Early follicle depletion during premenopause resulting in a lack of ovulation and thus lack of progesterone well before the onset of menopause

6. Exposure to xenoestrogens (cause of early follicle depletion)

Most women in the industrialized world now suffer from hormonal imbalance throughout each of the major life cycles—the childbearing years, perimenopause, menopause and post-menopause. In contrast, most women in other parts of the world—the Pacific Rim, Africa and South America...

1. Do not suffer from PMS

2. Do not experience degenerative symptoms of menopause—hot flashes, night sweats, vaginal dryness, bloating, weight gain, mood swings, headaches

3. Do not have the diseases that are now associated with postmenopause in the industrialized countries (osteoporosis, heart disease and memory loss)

While the foods we choose to eat and the exercises we choose to do play an important role in helping us maintain hormonal balance, environmental contaminants such as xenobiotics are a significant problem.

WHAT ARE XENOBIOTICS?

Xenobiotics are molecules from petrochemical sources that contaminate the environment, the food chain and the air that we breathe. They are all around us—in the out-gassing of carpet, spermicidal gels, spreading agents in salad dressings. Many of these substances act as estrogenic substances. Others are anti-estrogenic. The term *xenobiotic* is now used more often than *xenoestrogen* because it covers a wider field.

When molecules of these xenobiotics mimic the hormones in our bodies—estrogens, progesterone and others by occupying the same receptor sites as our endogenous hormones—we develop hormonal imbalance. Estrogen dominance is a key factor in degenerative disease. I recommend an excellent article in *Science News* magazine for an in-depth look at what researchers are discovering about environmental hormones—chemicals and pollutants that are "exerting a feminizing effect on the animal kingdom."[36]

We come in contact with xenoestrogens in food, particularly meat and dairy with the heavy concentration of pesticide residue. The beef that we produce in America is, in the opinion of many experts, a threat to the health and well-being of those who consume it. The following comments are from an article written by Dr. Samuel S. Epstein, professor of Environmental and Occupational Medicine at the University of Illinois School of Public Health in Chicago:

The question we ought to be asking is not why Europe

won't buy our hormone-treated meat, but why we allow beef from hormone-treated cattle to be sold to American and Canadian consumers...The endocrine-disruptive effects of estrogenic pesticides and other industrial food contaminants known as xenoestrogens are now under intensive investigation by federal regulatory agencies. But the contamination of meat with residues of the far more potent estradiol remains ignored.

These hormones are linked ever more closely to the escalating incidence of reproductive cancers in the U.S. since 1950—55 percent for breast cancer, 120 percent for testicular cancer, and 190 percent for prostate cancer.[37]

If we consume only organic meat and dairy, we eliminate the greatest source of xenoestrogens. Organic grass-fed beef is not only free from chemical contaminants, but it is also high in omega-3 fatty acids (as opposed to grain-fed beef, which is high in saturated fat).

Gasoline fumes and soft plastics are also sources of xenoestrogens. None of us should be subjected to gasoline fumes, and we should avoid being contaminated by plastics whenever possible. The clingy plastic wrap is the most hazardous. When we wrap our food with plastic, the chemicals in the plastic are absorbed by the food.

John R. Lee explains that the xenoestrogen will cause an inappropriate hormonal response or it will block the normal hormone response. When our receptors are filled with these antagonists, our natural hormones are unable to work properly.[38] If our diet does not contain plant estrogens such as the isoflavones found in soybeans or the lignans found in flaxseed, we have little protection from the xenoestrogens. The plant estrogens rescue us by occupying the estrogen receptor sites.

How are xenoestrogens affecting human beings? We are responding to these petrochemical derivatives the same way that the alligators in Florida are responding. Female alligators aren't making eggs. They have large ovaries and follicles that are not functioning. Young women in the United States are not making eggs and not making progesterone. This is why it is so important for even young women to have a hormone saliva test. A low level of progesterone could cause infertility, premenstrual syndrome, autoimmune disease, miscarriage, bone loss and many other disorders. Simple, noninvasive saliva testing is available.

Young girls are entering puberty at earlier and earlier ages due to estrogen dominance. Men have been affected as well. Males in industrialized countries are producing sperm at a rate that is 50 percent lower than the rate of sperm production thirty-five years ago. Babies may look normal, and then, when they reach their thirties, the females may lose the ability to make progesterone and the males the ability to make sperm. John Lee concludes:

> We have a dysfunctional conventional medicine based on chemically altered hormones—analogues—and the typical doctors only know about these. They don't even know that natural progesterone exists and yet it's been out in these creams for years.
>
> We have to tell people that there's a problem. Progesterone deficiency exists. Estrogen deficiency is largely a myth. The problems that women are mostly hampered by—osteoporosis, breast cancer, decline in mental acuity, loss of libido—these are related to progesterone. They are not estrogen problems.[39]

PROTOCOLS USING BIOIDENTICAL HORMONES

Those physicians who are more informed regarding the dangers of estrogens and estrogen dominance recommend bioidentical progesterone to women who are suffering hormonal imbalance during the childbearing years, perimenopause, menopause and postmenopause.

The benefits of using natural progesterone are explained in the following excerpt from a book by Neal Barnard, M.D.:

> During the normal monthly cycle, estrogen dominates during the first half of the month, causing the uterine lining to thicken in anticipation of pregnancy. During the second half of the month, a different hormone, progesterone, dominates. Among other jobs, progesterone opposes the actions of estrogen, preventing too much stimulation of the uterus.
>
> Progesterone is only made if you ovulate, i.e. an

ovary releases an egg. If that does not happen for what-ever reason, there is no progesterone to oppose estrogen.

In order to restore hormone balance, doctors sometimes prescribe synthetic progesterone derivatives (e.g. Provera). Unfortunately, they have a long list of side effects. An equally effective and much safer form is available without a prescription.

Natural progesterone is derived from yams or soy-beans, and is an exact duplicate of human proges-terone.[40]

Fifteen years of clinical practice proved to John Lee many truths about progesterone. He retired and wrote a book at the age of sixty "to shorten the learning curve for other people."[41] The book, *Natural Progesterone: The Multiple Roles of a Remarkable Hormone*, explains in technical, medical language everything he has learned about progesterone and hormonal balance. Lee's work cannot be dismissed or disputed.

Physicians who encounter John Lee's work know that they did not hear any of the information that John R. Lee is giving them in medical school, at conventional medical conventions or in text-books. They certainly are not going to get Lee's information from the pharmaceutical representatives or pharmaceutical publications. Consequently, many physicians found his work "very inflamma-tory." He was challenging what the pharmaceutical companies were saying. He was challenging what was being taught in medical school.[42]

A PROVEN TRACK RECORD

Yet, the track record of success that Dr. Lee's decades of hor-monal treatment with natural progesterone provide proves that use of natural progesterone is a valuable alternative to the prob-lematic ERT and HRT regimens.

For those women who are suffering from estrogen dominance, Dr. Lee recommends a low dose of natural progesterone (20 to 25 milligrams) twice a day. This is a physiologic dose. He also recom-mends that women be hormone free at least one week (five to seven days) per month. Otherwise, we risk reducing sensitivity at the hormone receptor sites. Dr. Lee recommends this protocol for women during perimenopause, menopause and postmenopause as needed. Many women find that they require a higher dose at different times of the month, or even for the entire twenty-one-day period each month.

My own progesterone needs have changed over the last four years, and in speaking to compounding pharmacists, I have discovered that many women are taking 50 to 100 milligrams of natural progesterone each day with excellent results.

NONINVASIVE, ACCURATE AND INEXPENSIVE SALIVA HORMONE TESTS

According to David T. Zava, Ph.D., expert in biomedical research, saliva is the best type of body fluid that we could use to test hormonal levels. He explains that saliva reflects the bioactive levels of endogenous hormones. It is more representative of what amount of hormone is biologically available to the target tissues of the body."[43]

Sex steroid hormone levels should be monitored. First, testing will establish the specific need regarding bioidentical hormone therapy, which is the only safe and effective form of hormone replacement therapy. Subsequent testing will verify that hormone levels are in the optimal range or establish a need to increase or decrease any of the sex steroid hormones being tested.

Routine hormone level measurements are an important part of optimal hormone therapy. Noninvasive tests, careful hormone saliva collection (simply done, with clear and easy-to-follow instructions) and accurate laboratory analysis measuring the free, unbound hormone levels will allow you to determine your sex steroid hormone needs.

Although testing may reveal that estrogen levels are low, it is unwise to begin taking even a bioidentical estrogen (such as bioidentical estriol) until the natural progesterone has had time to impact the body. This could be several weeks or several months. Progesterone, in the overwhelming majority of women, encourages the rise of estrogen, testosterone and corticosteroids to optimal levels.[44]

TERRY DORIAN RESOURCES

For information on purchasing hormone saliva test kits, bioidentical nonprescription progesterone and nutritional supplementation, go to www.terrydorian.com.

For the latest protocols for safe, effective bioidentical hormone replacement therapy, go to my ministry site at www.healthbeginsinhim.org.

Online I am able to provide the latest information and updates, as well as my personal recommendations concerning:

- Diagnostic laboratories

- Information and costs of noninvasive saliva hormone test kits that are supplied by each of the laboratories that I recommend

- Problems associated with the steroid hormones that have been studied most extensively in saliva, and the current protocols prescribed by integrative physicians using bioidentical hormones:

  - Estrogens (estradiol, estrone and estriol)

  - Progesterone—during the childbearing years, perimenopause, menopause, surgical menopause, postmenopause and as an important therapy for PMS and infertility

  - Androgens (DHEA, testosterone, DHT)

  - Cortisol

- Information on andropause (male menopause)

- Compounding pharmacies that I personally recommend

- My current workout regimen, nutritional supplement regimen and the specific protocols I follow to maintain hormonal balance

THE MIND-BODY CONNECTION

As we have discussed, diet and exercise are vital factors in maintaining optimal health, including hormonal balance. Supplemental nutrients and bioidentical hormone therapy are usually essential for those of us living in the Western industrialized world. However, hormonal balance and a healthy endocrine system also depend on how we react to the challenges of life. Responding with grace and dignity to the routine stresses in our lives requires more strength than we can humanly possess, but in Christ we possess all the strength we need.

Dr. Candace Pert, whom we met earlier, helps us understand this mind-body connection that includes the hormonal system:

> The point I am making is that your brain is extremely well integrated with the rest of your body at a molecular level, so much so that the term mobile brain is an apt description of the psychosomatic network through which intelligent information travels from one system to another. Every one of the zones, or systems, of the network—the neural, the hormonal, the gastrointestinal, and the immune—is set up to communicate with one another, via peptides and messenger-specific peptide receptors. Every second, a massive information exchange is occurring in your body. Imagine each of these messenger systems possessing a specific tone, humming a signature tune, rising and falling, body music with our ears, then the sum of these sounds would be the music that we call the emotions.[45]

As to the role of the mind, in connection with the health of our physical bodies, how very different our conscious thoughts are from God's thoughts. We would fail to reach any divine level of thinking, in spite of our best thoughts and actions. Then in Christ, we find that we are already rescued, because the Holy Spirit transcends all that we think or do. I frequently turn to Isaiah 55:8–12 for a reminder of this powerful truth:

> "My thoughts are completely different from yours," says the LORD. "And my ways are far beyond anything you could imagine. For just as the heavens are higher than the earth, so are my ways higher than your ways

and my thoughts higher than your thoughts.

"The rain and snow come down from the heavens and stay on the ground to water the earth. They cause the grain to grow, producing seed for the farmer and bread for the hungry. It is the same with my word. I send it out, and it always produces fruit. It will accomplish all I want it to, and it will prosper everywhere I send it. You will live in joy and peace."

As we turn our attention to this spiritual connection to consider how we heal in this vital dimension, I invite you to open your heart to receive a divine encounter with your God, Creator and Holy Spirit.

How We Heal

The Spiritual Connection

KEY QUESTIONS

1. How can I walk in wholeness?

2. What is the spiritual dimension of total health and restoration?

The study of health and healing touches more profound dimensions of life than most of us think when we first begin this journey. Although the words *health* and *healing* are familiar to everyone, most of us begin the journey to health and restoration very far from ever having known what it means to be physically, mentally, emotionally and spiritually whole.

What do I need to know in order to be whole? This is a question beyond the scope of a ten- or fifteen-minute visit with a doctor. *How do I find wholeness?* This question cannot be entirely answered by a health practitioner or a multidisciplinary team of health and healing professionals. Each of them can hand us pieces of information that they believe will be useful. *How do I find wholeness?* This is a fundamental question, a persistent question, but the answer is not found in a verbal explanation. Wholeness is a journey that we ourselves initiate as we discover the grace of God and the power of the Holy Spirit, our Creator and Savior.

Three elements of the spiritual dimension that are major determinants of health and healing are:

1. The desire to walk in faith, love, mercy and forgiveness

2. The will to change

3. The wisdom to seek God

SCIENCE CONFIRMS SPIRIT

During the last three decades of the twentieth century, the best biochemical researchers have proved irrefutably that the workings of the body and mind are inextricably linked. We now know that Descartes' seventeenth-century philosophy, as we discussed earlier, which separated the mind and body (mind-body dualism) and influenced four centuries of scientific reasoning, was hopelessly flawed. Yet, we are still reaping its profound effects.

Because of this faulty perception, scientists turned away from the biblical revelation of man as a triune being made in the image of a triune God. By insisting on viewing human beings as a mind-body entity, they lost the ancient wisdom concerning health and healing, wisdom based on the intricate body-mind-spirit connection. Instead, as Dr. Robert D. Orr, director of clinical bioethics at the Center for Christian Bioethics, explains:

> During the enlightenment, the Age of Reason of the 17th and 18th centuries, came great advances in the physical sciences and the development of a mechanistic view of human life. The human body came to be visualized as a machine that could be studied and understood, and occasionally the course of illness could be altered. At the same time, a shift in philosophical thought formulated the ideals of human dignity and worth which led to the centrality of mankind in the universe, with a coincident decrease in acknowledgement of the sovereignty of God leading to a veritable worship of Man's abilities. In the words of Paul as recorded in the first chapter of Romans, they "worshiped and served created things rather than the Creator."[46]

Now scientific research has clearly established that the well-being of the mind, soul and "spirit" must be included in any enlightened discussion concerning physical health. Many health professionals believe that the workings of the mind, emotions and spirit are indeed *central* to any discussion of health and healing.

Scientists now understand that our intelligence is not located only in the brain, but rather intelligence is "in the cells that are distributed throughout the body."[47] That means that how we think, feel, talk and believe sends a message to the body and "that the immune system, like the central nervous system has the capacity to learn."[48]

The vital message to those seeking optimal health and fitness is that the Bible, along with the most informed research in brain biochemistry, clearly establishes the mind-body-spirit connection. What we think and feel, our deepest convictions and our most intense emotions, have the power to change our bodies at the molecular level.

We are not simply talking about thoughts that lead to decisions to consume the best foods and implement other healthful lifestyle choices. What we decide to do in terms of dietary and lifestyle activities is only one aspect of health and healing. Who we are mentally, who we are emotionally and who we are spiritually become the overarching components of health and healing. The staggering reality is that on a moment-by-moment basis, our thoughts and emotions communicate with every system in the body, including the immune system, neurological system and digestive system.

THE ROLE OF THE SPIRIT IN SCRIPTURE

The Scriptures reveal that God created us as phenomenal human beings with three separately discernible aspects of our humanity—a body, a soul (mind, will and emotions) and a spirit. We can be considered as tripartite beings. While it is not within the scope of this manuscript to discuss thoroughly this reality, the following verses of Scripture allude to this truth:

> And the LORD God formed man of the dust of the ground, and breathed into his nostrils the breath of life; and man became a living soul.
>
> **—GENESIS 2:7, KJV**

The word *breath* in Genesis 2:7 is derived from the Hebrew word *neshamah,* which means "divine inspiration" and can be translated "soul" or "spirit." In the Book of Proverbs, *neshama* is translated as "spirit."

> The spirit of man is the lamp of the LORD, searching all the innermost parts of his being.
>
> **—PROVERBS 20:27, NAS**

The Old Testament prophet Zechariah confirmed the work of the Creator in forming the spirit of man:

> This message is from the LORD, who stretched out the heavens, laid the foundations of the earth, and formed the spirit within humans.
>
> **—ZECHARIAH 12:1**

In the New Testament, the apostle Paul refers to the work of God that will make us whole—spirit, soul and body:

> Now may the God of peace make you holy in every way, and may your whole spirit and soul and body be kept blameless until that day when our Lord Jesus

Christ comes again. God, who calls you, is faithful; he
will do this.

—1 THESSALONIANS 5:23–24

This wonderful prayer reveals God's will for us to know His peace and wholeness for our entire being—spirit, soul and body. When Jesus was on earth, He shared with His disciples how this wonderful promise could be ours:

> But now I am going away to the one who sent me...it
> is actually best for you that I go away, because if I don't,
> the Counselor won't come. If I do go away, he will
> come because I will send him to you...When the Spirit
> of truth comes, he will guide you into all truth.
>
> —JOHN 16:5, 7, 13

Scripture teaches us that we honor God as we yield to the power of the Holy Spirit, who will teach us and lead us into all truth. As followers of Christ who allow the Word of God to renew our minds, we learn how to yield our entire lives to the Holy Spirit, who gives us the power to become whole.

Only by the power of the Holy Spirit do we begin to recognize that abundance, loss, blessing, betrayal, wisdom, folly, knowledge, ignorance, faith, fear, courage, recklessness, holiness, lust, forgiveness, bitterness, humility, pride, meekness, arrogance, fertility, barrenness, hope, despair, love, hate, peace and anxiety—are all our teachers on the journey to wholeness. We don't know what it means to be whole until we see Christ as the Source of everything we need for life. Wholeness becomes possible only when we find our identity—solely and completely—in Christ.

God-given teachers on the journey to wholeness help us put our personal health and healing challenges in proper perspective. Some of those teachers we probably recognize better as life circumstances that cause us big trouble. We are tempted to react violently against them. Others we recognize as heroes, bigger-than-life people who transcend the smallness of many people and accomplish great things with their lives.

TEACHERS OF THE SPIRIT

As we acknowledge the complex interaction of body-mind-spirit, we first have to reckon with what we have been taught to be our personal world-view. You may not have considered that you even have a world-view or understand what that involves. Yet, each of us will define *spirit* according to our world-view, whether we do so consciously or unconsciously. For a brief comparison of the most prevalent modern world-views, please turn to the appendix and view the World-view Comparison Chart. Consider which one you relate to most easily. Does your view of life reflect the philosophy of naturalism, transcendentalism, theism or a biblical world-view?

The important thing to remember is that when all people have the freedom to define *spirit,* that includes those who have a biblical world-view. Only recently have Christian physicians been welcomed in the mind-body discussion, and they are indeed leading the way through people like Harold Koenig, M.D. of the Center for the Study of Religion, Spirituality and Health at Duke University and Dale Mathews, M.D., associate professor of medicine at Georgetown University.

Perhaps the best answer to modern, godless philosophies for those who share, as I do, a biblical world-view is found in two passages from the New Testament that explain the source of their error:

> But people who aren't Christians can't understand these truths from God's Spirit. It all sounds foolish to them because only those who have the Spirit can understand what the Spirit means.
>
> **—1 CORINTHIANS 2:14**

> All Scripture is inspired by God and is useful to teach us what is true and to make us realize what is wrong in our lives. It straightens us out and teaches us to do what is right. It is God's way of preparing us in every way, fully equipped for every good thing God wants us to do.
>
> **—2 TIMOTHY 3:16–17**

No final balm, no antiaging strategy, no wise physician or non-physician health practitioner, no human love or friendship can meet the deepest need within each of us to know our Creator and to be known, loved, forgiven, accepted, celebrated and protected by our precious Lord. How then do we find Him? We need a revelation of Jesus Christ as our Lord and Savior, our Healer and our Friend.

God has not asked us to create or to contrive in our own strength the life that is only possible by the power of the Holy Spirit. We cannot walk in love, mercy and wisdom until our lives are securely resting in the love of Christ. For that to happen, we must cry out humbly and passionately to God that we cannot live without Him!

By the power of the Spirit, we long for God, even before we know we are searching for Jesus. A longing for more becomes a quest for more, and seeking love, meaning and immortality becomes bigger than our hearts can bear. Often through adversity, always through prayer and completely by grace, we receive, by the power of the Holy Spirit, the freedom and unction to walk in mercy. The apostle Paul tells us precisely how spiritual reality happens:

> Now, the Lord is the Spirit, and wherever the Spirit of the Lord is, he gives freedom. And all of us have had that veil removed so that we can be mirrors that brightly reflect the glory of the Lord. And as the Spirit of the Lord works within us, we become more and more like Him and reflect his glory even more.
> —2 CORINTHIANS 3:17–18

THE APOSTLE PAUL, A BIBLICAL HERO

We become new creatures in Christ through a revelation of Him. God makes a way for us where there is no way. He gives us the power of the Holy Spirit to do what we can only do in His strength! The apostle Paul learned this truth by a life-changing experience as dramatic as any person before or after him. A persecutor and murderer of Christians, he was changed and called by God to discover what it means to live in Christ and to walk by the power of the Holy Spirit. He taught fellow Christians how to live in love, joy, peace, faith, hope and fulfillment while experiencing ongoing pain, betrayal, danger, hardship and multifarious adversities. His writings show us today the path to healing and wholeness.

From Paul's encounter, we can learn never to assume that any meeting is incidental, or that any moment of our lives is without meaning or the potential for greatness. Traveling with his companions, fixed on the plan to persecute believers in Damascus, Saul of Tarsus (later called Paul) had a personal encounter with

Christ. Knocked from his horse and blinded by the brilliant light he encountered, this religious murderer could only cry out, "Who are You, Lord?" (Acts 9:5, NKJV).

Countless Christians from that day until the present have gone through similar awakenings, suddenly receiving just such a "revelation in Christ." We call it a "Damascus Road experience" because there is no better way to describe the blinding light that burns the scales from our spiritual eyes and gives us the power to see Jesus Christ for who He is—our Lord and Savior.

Saul of Tarsus, the arch-enemy of the fledgling new church, became the apostle Paul, called to suffer for Christ and to establish and encourage the church through all the ages with his revelation of his beloved Master. The Pauline epistles, contained in the New Testament, take us from our fallen state into an understanding of salvation in Christ, lift us beyond a life of carnality and lead us to our destiny in Christ. (See Romans 10:9–10; Ephesians 2:4–6; 3:16–20.)

While the apostle Paul is a startling example of the power of God to transform our lives completely and cause us to fulfill our divine destiny, there are many in modern history as well who can provoke us to seek the righteousness of Christ. One of my heroes and one of the most courageous women in American history was Harriet Tubman. Nicknamed "Moses," Harriet escaped slavery and risked her life again and again by returning to the South to rescue others.

Harriet Tubman, a nineteenth-century hero

As a woman, I cannot think of a better hero for women than Harriet Tubman, who was born in 1820 and lived to be ninety-four years old. She moved through adversity with great abandon to the Lord, walking in courage, determination, perseverance, self-denial and faith.

Harriet was born in Dorchester County, Maryland, on the Brodas Plantation. The owner produced lumber and "raised" slaves to rent or sell. One of eleven children, Harriet had the good fortune to be raised by her mother at a time when plantation owners frequently sold off the children of their slaves. She lived with her family in a one-room shack without windows. She had few clothes and wore the same soiled dress day after day.

Her family's dwelling did not provide adequate protection from the cold, and a resourceful Harriet often covered her toes in smoldering ashes to prevent frostbite. She endured the routine hardships of slave life and suffered many beatings as a child. She ran away at the age of seven. She said in an interview after the Civil War, "I stayed from Friday till de nex' Cheusday, fightin' wid dose little pigs for de potato peelin's an oder scraps. By Chuesday I was so starved I knowed I'd got to go back to my Missus, I hadn't got no whar else to go."[49] At the age of twelve, she refused to assist in tying up a fellow slave who had tried to escape. Consequently, the man escaped to freedom. The owner retaliated by hitting Harriet in the head with a two-pound weight. She went into a coma, and it took months for her to recover from the nearly fatal injury. She reportedly suffered narcoleptic seizures and severe headaches for the rest of her life because of that injury.

In 1844, Harriet's master forced her to marry John Tubman, a free African American. Harriet remained a slave, but she was allowed to stay in Tubman's cabin at night. Then, as she had feared, the owner of the plantation died, and she heard that the slaves were to be sold. She planned her escape that night without telling her husband. John Tubman had been unfaithful to her on many occasions and threatened to tell the master if she tried to escape. She knew he would expose her.

Harriet Tubman not only made the ninety-mile trip to freedom, but she also became one of the most famous "conductors" of the Underground Railroad, a network of people who helped slaves escape from the South by providing the directions and transportation that moved them from contact to contact on the journey to freedom.

Harriet Tubman returned to Maryland again and again, leading over three hundred persons to freedom in the North. Her fearless acts of kindness while protecting those in her charge inspired awe. She continually expressed her confidence in God. When questioned about her amazing life, she said simply, "Twant me, twas the Lord. I always told him, 'I trust to you. I don't know where to go or what to do, but I expect you to lead me,' and he always did."

Later, during the Civil War, she served as a spy, a scout and a cook for the Union Army; she "earned the distinction as the only woman in American military history to plan and execute an armed expedition against enemy forces."[50]

ALBERT SCHWEITZER, A TWENTIETH-CENTURY HERO

A medical missionary to Africa for fifty years, a Nobel prize winner and a humanitarian claimed by ethical humanists as a soul mate, Schweitzer dedicated his life to modeling the ethical teachings of Jesus as recorded in the Gospels, particularly Matthew 25:31–46.

A theologian, philosopher, concert organist and physician, he left the comforts of a world that was eager to showcase his giftedness and reward his genius to establish a hospital at Lambarene, Gabon, French West Africa in 1913. He entered a harsh, forbidding environment with the will to serve others and to make a difference in their lives. Schweitzer held that the life of Jesus, the "ethic" of Jesus was the only thing in the world worth living. He dedicated his life to that end for fifty years of sojourns in Gabon.

When he writes of Jesus and the apostle Paul, it is with awe and reverence, honoring their lives because they so truly lived their "ethic." He imitated what he perceived to be the "ethic" of Jesus and the "ethic" of the apostle Paul. Although we honor Schweitzer's dedication, sensitivity, compassion, love and physical energy, we must note that it is impossible to embrace the ethic of Christ without acknowledging His role as God with us. And the ethic of the apostle Paul cannot be imitated without grasping his revelation of Christ and his faith in the resurrection power of the Lord.

Sadly, Schweitzer believed that neither modern science nor Christian theology could explain the universe. Considering Schweitzer's resolve to do what good he could in the lives of so many, in spite of his certainty that no divine plan, order or meaning for the world exists, seems to me a very great challenge to those of us who embrace a biblical world-view. If we know the Lord and trust Him as the Author and Finisher of our faith, how can we profess to walk in His light and eternal love and do less than one who is clinging desperately to the "ethic" of a man named Jesus—one he believed to be good but not divine?

What then is the one regrettable message that we find in Albert Schweitzer's life? Simply stated, it is the tragedy of embracing the ethic of Christ and disavowing the divinity of Christ. Without the divinity of Christ, we cannot transcend a world of wickedness, pain and violence. Without an understanding of God's purpose for humankind, we are left with the horror of a world void of meaning and created by chance. Without a personal Savior (as opposed to a life force) who knows us intimately and who can be known, there is no relief from loneliness or deliverance from guilt.

Perhaps the most powerful message of Albert Schweitzer's life is delivered in what he *did not* say or do. According to Jesus' own words, "This is what God wants you to do: Believe in the one he has sent" (John 6:29). Jesus clearly declared His divinity in this passage and others, referring to Himself as the true bread from heaven (v. 32). Yet, Schweitzer embraced the "ethic" of Christ without professing to accept Him as Lord.

Albert Schweitzer demonstrated a profound reverence for life and a commitment to support life and to relieve human suffering. He is responsible for the philosophy known as Reverence for Life. Through his life work, we see an enormous capacity to love and a desire to imitate the life of Jesus, together with a heart-wrenching lack of faith and trust in the God of Scripture who knows us and who wants to be known. One can only hope that at some point, even though it has not been recorded by history, he had a revelation of his Creator and Savior and that he experienced the unspeakable joy of knowing that all of life has a purpose and a plan, and that we can spend an eternity in the presence of the Lord Jesus Christ.

JACK MCCONNELL, M.D., A TWENTY-FIRST-CENTURY HERO

Nationally recognized scientist and medical researcher who retired at the age of sixty-four to a life of luxury and leisure on Hilton Head Island, South Carolina, Dr. McConnell soon discovered a hunger unsatisfied by success and ease. A few years after retiring, he had an "awakening" that moved him to dedicate his considerable training, talents and experience to a very noble cause. Dr. McConnell spearheaded a gargantuan effort to provide free, primary healthcare and a "culture of caring" to the "working poor." These individuals earn enough to disqualify themselves from Medicaid, but not enough to afford medical insurance for themselves and their families. He envisioned a clinic giving health professionals and lay volunteers the opportunity to donate their time and skills in a privately funded, debt-free enterprise.

The first permanent facility for the Volunteers in Medicine (VIM) Clinic opened its doors in 1994, fully staffed by retired physicians, nurses, dentists and chiropractors as well as nearly 150 lay volunteers. In 1994, the VIM Clinic had five thousand patient visits; by 2000, they had sixteen thousand. By 2002, at the age of seventy-seven, Jack McConnell's sixty-plus hours of unpaid labor each week had become his "new life work."

Where did the dream, the ethic, the consciousness that gives birth to such a life-impacting project originate? How did it become the desire of his heart? During my telephone conversations with Jack McConnell, I heard the answers to my questions in the unfolding story of his life. His responses to my inquiries revealed humility, humor, wisdom, transparency, kindness and the indomitable resolve to make life better for other people. Some dreams are in the making for more than a lifetime. Jack's vision and faith were born in the heart of his father. The kindness and compassion of Jack's parents had clearly become the language of his life.

Jack's dad, a Methodist minister who never earned more than $150 per month in his life, changed the lives of others by the words he spoke and lived. He and his wife were each born in the log cabins that their parents had built. To the twenty-first-century American mind, Jack's parents lived in dire poverty. However, in spite of the grim and austere setting, it was hardly impoverished. The seven children were nurtured and reared to help each other fulfill their dreams. They later earned seven bachelor degrees, three master degrees and four doctorates. The father helped the oldest child, the oldest child and the father helped the next child, and then each child helped the other until every child had a degree. Caring and sharing, a routine part of life in the McConnell home, characterized their lives.

Jack was raised in the coal mining community of Crumpler, West Virginia, located thirty-five miles northwest of Bluefield. Jack spent his early childhood in the parsonage next door to the church, the last house in the hollow. If you saw the film *October Sky,* you have experienced something of the look, feel and sound of Crumpler. Coal dust permeated the air. Jack remembers playing on the black lawn as a young child and laughs. "I didn't think it was bad. I thought it was normal."

During the Depression, Jack's parents often served lunch to forty or fifty people. Their front gate had been "marked," and people in need of food knew that they could get a meal there. The family had a big garden with lots of corn and tomatoes, and they could always find a chicken somewhere.

They never had a car. His dad always said he could not "support Mr. Ford" on a minister's salary. They walked everywhere or hitched rides. Life for Jack, the youngest of seven children, was always filled with good fun, people from church and, most of all, wonderful times around the family table at dinner. The wisdom of his father, casually imparted in an atmosphere of joy and good will, touched his soul.

The most important business of the McConnell household occurred once the children got home from school or other activities. The family gathered around the dining-room table and took turns answering their father's question: "And what did you do for someone today?" Years later, after Jack finished school and began his career, he continued to hear that question in soft echoes, and to see the larger-than-life images of his father walking out the reality of Matthew 25:33–40.

Jack McConnell completed postgraduate training in pediatrics at Baylor College of Medicine and attended Harvard and Columbia Business Schools. Then he went on to make notable contributions to our country as a physician, researcher, teacher, inventor, administrator and humanitarian. Here are a few of his notable achievements:

- He invented and directed the development of the TB Tine Test, which is used in the diagnosis of tuberculosis.

- He directed the development of Tylenol tablets.

- He directed the development of the first commercial MRI system in the United States.

- He wrote the Senate bill authoring the Human Genome Program and cofounded the Institute for Genomic Research.

Dr. McConnell's vitae—offering a full list of honors, accomplishments, memberships and acts of service—reveal a life that is marked not only by what the world counts as achievement and success, but also as a man dedicated to service.

After retirement, he and his wife, Mary Ellen, built a home in one of the gated communities on Hilton Head Island, South Carolina, which is, of course, surrounded by yacht clubs and golf courses. He confessed that it didn't take long until he felt as though he were "sitting in nothing land." What began to capture his attention was the lifestyle of the native islanders.

Remembering always what it was like growing up without a car, he had developed a lifelong habit of giving rides to hitchhikers. In the course of many conversations with "local folks" who needed rides, he learned about life on the island. He discovered that the people who actually make the island work (e.g., gardeners, construction workers, maids and waitresses) had little or no access to healthcare. He felt outraged and wondered why someone didn't do something about that! Then he heard the words of his father again, not echoing softly, but ringing in his head: "What did you do for someone today?"[51] Stirred by the need and by his father's lifelong motivating "question," Jack McConnell developed a mental model for the Volunteers in Medicine Clinic in which the administration staff, professional staff and lay volunteers create a *Circle of Caring* as the heart and soul of the clinic. They decided to be guided by two life principles, both found in the New Testament: "Do unto others as you would have them do unto you," and "Love your neighbor as yourself."

They realized that by perceiving those they served as friends and neighbors, they would treat them with dignity, competence, care and compassion. Then by treating patients with dignity, competence, care and compassion, they would be perceived by the patients and the community as friends and neighbors indeed. The mission statement for the VIM Clinic grew out of the devotional life of Jack and Mary Ellen McConnell. Dr. McConnell says this prayer is not only the vision statement of the VIM Clinic, but is also the guide by which he lives his life:

> May we have eyes to see those rendered invisible and excluded, open arms and hearts to reach out and include them, healing hands to touch their lives with love, and in the process, heal ourselves.

News about the Volunteers in Medicine Clinic has spread. Retired physicians from all over the country call asking how they can start VIM Clinics in their communities. The *Volunteers in Medicine Institute,* a 501 (c) (3) nonprofit institute founded by Dr. McConnell, was established to assist individuals, hospitals, organizations or communities in the development of free health clinics— clinics whose mission is the delivery of healthcare to the medically underserved. As of June 2001, fifteen other VIM Clinics had begun operating, and they could not keep up with requests for help in organizing and funding more clinics. Dr. McConnell's evaluation of the clinics is: "The most distinct characteristic of the Volunteers in Medicine organization is its commitment to caring."

FINDING WHOLENESS IN SPIRIT

We have briefly outlined the importance of reckoning with your world-view, the impact your attitudes and thoughts have on your health and the satisfying life that awaits those who transcend their selfishness and learn to give life to others. All wholeness comes from God, and our ability to find God and cultivate a relationship with Him will determine the quality of our lives.

As you prepare to make important life decisions over the next six months, I encourage you to determine to focus on the spirit-mind-body connection. Ask God to reveal Himself to you in new ways that will allow you to experience the wonderful life He intended you to live.

How We Heal
Exercise Needed to Restore Your Body, Mind and Spirit

KEY QUESTION

1. How do various types of physical conditioning rebuild and strengthen the body, restore mobility, reverse aging and optimize mental and emotional health?

This is an introduction to our exercise program fully outlined in Part Four. The schedule of exercises provided enables us to restore and recondition our bodies—starting at any level and at any age—and offers a wonderful way to maintain the temple of the Holy Spirit. Martha Kimbel, my friend and fitness trainer in Atlanta, Georgia, designed this program based on my protocol for therapeutic conditioning.

Before you begin that important part of your journey to total health and restoration, it will be helpful to understand what part the various exercises play in optimizing your total well-being. Let the following quote inspire you:

> If doctors could prescribe exercise in pill form, it would be the single most widely prescribed drug in the world.
> **—ROBERT BUTLER, M.D.,**
> **FOUNDING DIRECTOR OF THE**
> **NATIONAL INSTITUTE ON AGING**

AEROBIC EXERCISE FOR MENTAL AND EMOTIONAL HEALTH

It has been established by research that physical exercise has a more powerful effect on mind, mood and emotions than does medication. Duke University announced the results of an important study early in 2001, a randomized clinical trial called the "SMILE" (Standard Medical Intervention and Long-Term Exercise). The study revealed that exercise reduced depression as effectively as medication in older adults (fifty years and older).

Each of the 150 people in the study met criteria for MDD (major depressive disorder) and were randomly selected to be in one of three groups: 1) exercise, 2) medication or 3) exercise and medication. Upon entry into the program, levels of depression did not differ significantly among the treatment groups. After four months, among those who no longer met criteria for MDD, those treated only with exercise did just as well as those treated with exercise and medication and those who had medication alone. The results are clear: Exercise is as potent in overcoming major depressive disorder as medication.[52]

THE BODY'S NATURAL OPIATES

Three years after Candace B. Pert discovered the opiate receptor in a human brain (October 25, 1972), a Scottish research team found the natural opiate, the brain's own morphine, "an endogenous ligand that fit the opiate receptor and created the same effects that morphine did."[53] That endogenous morphine was named "endorphin" by American researchers, and their name stuck.

Think about this. Morphine is a drug that produces intense pleasure and can relieve the most intense pain (at a high cost and with deadly consequences!). Yet, there is a natural opiate available to us free, in a completely safe and healthy version! Dr. Candace B. Pert made that discovery while she was at the National Institutes of Health. She designed a test that could measure levels of endorphins in the blood and conducted experiments that determined which kinds of behavior made the endorphin levels go up and which behaviors made them go down.

In animal studies (hamsters), they found that blood endorphin levels increased by about 200 percent from the beginning to the end of the sex act. Next, they took blood samples from psychiatrists at National Institutes of Health who were serious runners. That too established a definite increase in endorphins as a result of the exercise. Dr. Pert and Peter Ferrell, an exercise physiologist, co-authored the first published study that provided "physiological validation of the phenomenon we now know as runners' high."[54]

I now experience that regular endorphin high when I cycle each day on my stationary Schwinn Johnny G Spinner Pro while looking across the meadow, watching the news or listening to music. For me, that comes after about forty-five minutes of exercise when I am soaked with sweat.

In addition to the benefits of aerobic exercise for those with major depressive disorder and anxiety, cardiorespiratory fitness can lead to a 15 percent improvement in mental tests. Testing was done on volunteers aged from sixty to seventy-five, most of whom had not done any formal exercise for over thirty or forty years.[55] It is never too late to exercise. For the next six months, the researchers did something different. Half of the volunteers took long walks while the other half did toning exercises using weights, as well as stretching exercises. The strength and flexibility training did nothing for their mental abilities.[64]

When we aren't aerobically fit, the heart has to pump hard to get oxygen to the muscle. That stresses the body and raises the heart rate. No pill, dietary supplement, food—not even the best dietary regimen—can replace the power of aerobic exercise. The endorphin response to rigorous aerobic exercise is an incredible reward for diligence to exercise daily. Eating right and exercise must accompany each other in order to achieve optimal health.

REDUCING CORTISOL LEVELS = REDUCING STRESS

Endorphin release also reduces the levels of cortisol in the bloodstream. Cortisol is the hormone we are most apt to produce in toxic quantities when we are responding to life events with intense stress. Cortisol production at higher than normal levels creates insulin resistance, a major cause of obesity, heart disease and Type 2 diabetes in the United States.

Aerobic activity reduces stress and helps overcome Type 2 diabetes, heart disease and obesity—not only by burning calories, but by making our bodies more sensitive to insulin. All of us want to improve our insulin sensitivity, as we have discussed, because it is the number one determinant of how fast we age.

No matter how little you want to exercise or how few minutes you feel like exercising—just start. The healthiest people in the world exercise throughout the day, seven days a week. What day of the week wouldn't we want to experience the power of endorphins? Keep dancing, jumping, walking, bicycling, swimming or running for some portion of each day.

On our 180-Day Journey, you choose the aerobic activities you like. Just begin to exercise aerobically every day.

STRENGTH TRAINING FOR ENERGY

Weight training builds bone, increases our energy, improves balance and makes us more flexible. On our 180-Day Journey, we strength train four days a week, two days for the upper body and two days for the lower body. We continue to burn fat after we exercise, simply by building muscle. Our strength-training instructions feature two photographs of Martha in a beginning and ending position for each exercise. The instructions are easy to follow. With only ten exercises, you will be working every major muscle group.

Go as slowly with the weights as you need to go. Again, just start. It doesn't matter where you start. Every day you will be moving forward, strengthening muscles that once were weak. Think about what you want to be when you are sixty, eighty, one hundred or one hundred twenty years old. We are wonderfully made. We can heal. We can be strong.

RESTORING AND MAINTAINING FLEXIBILITY

On the island of Okinawa people enjoy greater health and longevity than most people in the world. Researchers are just beginning to look at their health-promoting lifestyle and culture.

Imagine sitting with a group of Okinawan elders who are all over one hundred years old. They are seated cross-legged on the floor, and they sit in that position for hours. Such flexibility is a result of the fact that they have kept moving and stretching all of their lives. It is never too late.

Those who live in sedentary societies, such as the United States, often show signs of aging very early in life. For example, a great many people in their late twenties or thirties already have muscles that have begun to shrink and joints that are not very limber. Flexibility is expected of children and perhaps teens, but not long into adulthood.

Many people think of flexibility training as a vital part of warmup in order to reduce the likelihood of injury. Stretching is essential in signaling to the body that muscles will be in need of an increase in oxygen. However, it is much more than that.

The Okinawans are an example of what flexibility training can produce. People in their eighties, nineties and older are able to move with the same agility and grace as people half their age. That kind of flexibility offers enormous benefits for our health. Stretching properly and for a sufficient period of time each day feels as good as having a massage.

Some people will want to rotate the stretches. Others, like myself, do all the stretches every day. The only way that I can sit for long hours at the computer is to exercise vigorously and stretch for at least an hour, often more, a day.

As we lengthen and strengthen muscles, our stretching massage is a wonderful way to begin and to close each day. Listening to recorded music and Scripture can also help to make the time meaningful. Here are some of the important benefits of the daily stretches in our 180-Day Journey.

- Stretching sends an increased blood supply and nutrients to the joints. By increasing the temperature of the tissue, circulation increases and nutrients are more easily transported.

- Stretching increases joint synovial fluid and promotes the transport of nutrients to the joints' cartilage, giving us a greater range of motion and reducing joint degeneration.

- Stretching reduces low back pain by relaxing the muscles. Contracted muscles require more work to accomplish activities.

- Stretching makes it less likely that muscles will tighten, thus it reduces fatigue.

- Neuromuscular coordination is improved with stretching, helping opposing muscle groups to work more synergistically.

UNDERSTANDING "YOUR EXERCISE PROGRAM"

The Flexibility Training exercises on page 224 each have a photo to show you the correct posture. I suggest you mark a monthly calendar to help you follow a seven-day rotation of stretches, a seven-day aerobic schedule and a four-day-a-week strength-training schedule.

The Strength Training exercises (page 221) show you how to increase weights over a six-month period and guide you through a safe regimen of increasing repetitions. Everyone needs to progress at a rate that feels very comfortable.

Done correctly, aerobic exercise, strength training and flexibility training all bring enormous pleasure and relaxation to you—body, soul and spirit. Exercise time can be a time for games and play. It can also be a time of quiet and solitude.

For Those With Special Challenges

Life may have brought you into a situation that seems impossible to face, much less overcome. The love of God and the counsel of the Holy Spirit can help you to confront impossible odds and learn to walk in the optimal health you desire. To those who face special challenges and insurmountable difficulties, I offer this famous prayer:

> I asked for strength that I might achieve;
> I was made weak that I might learn humbly to obey.
> I asked for health that I might do greater things;
> I was given infirmity that I might do better things.
> I asked for riches that I might be happy;
> I was given poverty that I might be wise.
> I asked for power that I might have the praise of men;
> I was given weakness that I might feel the need of God.
> I asked for all things that I might enjoy life;
> I was given life that I might enjoy all things.
> I got nothing that I had asked for
> But everything that I had hoped for.
> Almost despite myself my unspoken prayers were answered;
> I am, among all men, most richly blessed.

—PRAYER OF AN UNKNOWN CONFEDERATE SOLDIER

Regardless of life's challenges, maintain a positive attitude and outlook on life. Exercise and eat the proper foods, and soon you will begin to experience total healing and restoration.

Part Four

A 180–Day Journey

YOU ARE GETTING READY TO BEGIN an exciting, life-changing journey toward *Total Health and Restoration.* I have prepared for you a six-month outline of what should be happening during those 180 days in order for you to reach your desired destination.

Of course, you will be gaining understanding from the materials you have read concerning lifestyle and how foods heal, especially as they apply to your specific condition. You will need to make the effort to change any lifestyle habits that have been destructive to your health to this point. Beyond that, as you determine to follow this guide for the next 180 days, you will cultivate new, life-giving habits that will lead you to health and wholeness.

Each of the six month sections will provide you with a selection of foods that you need to incorporate into your diet, exercises that will strengthen and heal your body and a daily verse of Scripture and "Milestone" marker that will help to renew your mind and spirit. Taking small steps to wholeness is not difficult. You only need to make a decision and then begin. Are you ready?

Milestone One

We Seek His Way

*The love of Christ and His Word in our hearts
cause us to seek His way and enable us to hear His voice.*

Vision

OUR GREATEST HOPE FOR CHANGE begins with the knowledge that each of us, as children of God, finds our identity in Him. Through His grace, His mercy and His love, we exchange our lives for His. The Word promises that His strength is made perfect in our weakness and that all things are possible to those who believe.

Spiritual Regimen

Living Each Hour in His Power

People Converted by Christ

DAY 1—ANDREW

Then John said, "I saw the Holy Spirit descending like a dove from heaven and resting upon him. I didn't know he was the one, but when God sent me to baptize with water, he told me, 'When you see the Holy Spirit descending and resting upon someone, he is the one you are looking for. He is the one who baptizes with the Holy Spirit.' I saw this happen to Jesus, so I testify that he is the Son of God."...Andrew, Simon Peter's brother, was one of these men who had heard what John said and then followed Jesus.

—*JOHN 1:32–34, 40*

DAY 2—PETER

Then Andrew brought Simon to meet Jesus. Looking intently at Simon, Jesus said, "You are Simon, the son of John—but you will be called Cephas" (which means Peter).

—*JOHN 1:42*

DAY 3—PHILIP

The next day Jesus decided to go to Galilee. He found Philip and said to him, "Come, be my disciple."

—*JOHN 1:43*

DAY 4—NATHANAEL

"Nazareth!" exclaimed Nathanael. "Can anything good come from there?" "Just come and see for yourself," Philip said. As they approached Jesus said, "Here comes an honest man—a true son of Israel." "How do you know about me?" Nathanael asked. And Jesus replied, "I could see you under the fig tree before Philip found you." Nathanael replied, "Teacher, you are the Son of God—the King of Israel!"

—JOHN 1:46–49

DAY 5—NICODEMUS

Jesus replied, "I assure you, unless you are born again, you can never see the Kingdom of God." "What do you mean?" exclaimed Nicodemus. "How can a man go back into his mother's womb and be born again?" Jesus replied, "The truth is, no one can enter the Kingdom of God without being born of water and the Spirit."

—JOHN 3:3–5

DAY 6—THE SAMARITAN WOMAN

Jesus replied, "People soon become thirsty again after drinking this water. But the water I give them takes away thirst altogether. It becomes a perpetual spring within them, giving them eternal life." "Please, sir," the woman said, "give me some of that water!"

— JOHN 4:13–15

DAY 7—A NOBLEMAN

The official pleaded, "Lord, please come now before my little boy dies." Then Jesus told him, "Go back home. Your son will live!" And the man believed Jesus' word and started home. While he was on his way, some of the servants met him with the news that his son was alive and well. He asked them when the boy had begun to feel better, and they replied, "Yesterday afternoon at one o'clock his fever suddenly disappeared!" Then the father realized it was the same time that Jesus had told him, "Your son will live." And the officer and his entire household believed in Jesus.

—JOHN 4:49–53

DAY 8—An adulterous woman

Then Jesus stood up again and said to her, "Where are your accusers? Didn't even one of them condemn you?" "No, Lord," she said. And Jesus said, "Neither do I. Go and sin no more."

—John 8:10–11

DAY 9—A blind man

"Why, that's very strange!" the man replied. "He healed my eyes, and yet you don't know anything about him! Well, God doesn't listen to sinners, but he is ready to hear those who worship him and do his will. Never since the world began has anyone been able to open the eyes of someone born blind. If this man were not from God, he couldn't do it."... "You have seen him," Jesus said, "and he is speaking to you!" "Yes, Lord," the man said, "I believe!" And he worshiped Jesus.

—John 9:30–33, 37–38

DAY 10—Martha

"Yes, Lord," she told him. "I have always believed you are the Messiah, the Son of God, the one who has come into the world from God."

—John 11:27

DAY 11—A centurion

Then the officer said, "Lord, I am not worthy to have you come into my home. Just say the word from where you are, and my servant will be healed!"...When Jesus heard this, he was amazed. Turning to the crowd, he said, "I tell you the truth, I haven't seen faith like this in all the land of Israel!"...Then Jesus said to the Roman officer, "Go on home. What you have believed has happened."

—Matthew 8:8, 10, 13

DAY 12—Matthew

As Jesus was going down the road, he saw Matthew sitting at his tax-collection booth. "Come, be my disciple," Jesus said to him. So Matthew got up and followed him.

—Matthew 9:9

DAY 13—A Syrophoenician woman

A Gentile woman who lived there came to him, pleading, "Have mercy on me, O Lord, Son of David! For my daughter has a demon in her, and it is severely tormenting her." But Jesus gave her no reply—not even a word. Then his disciples urged him to send her away. "Tell her to leave," they said. "She is bothering us with all her begging." Then he said to the woman, "I was sent only to help the people of Israel—God's lost sheep—not the Gentiles." But she came and worshiped him and pleaded again, "Lord, help me!" "It isn't right to take food from the children and throw it to the dogs," he said. "Yes, Lord," she replied, "but even dogs are permitted to eat crumbs that fall beneath their master's table." "Woman," Jesus said to her, "your faith is great. Your request is granted." And her daughter was instantly healed.

—Matthew 15:22-28

DAY 14—A demoniac from the land of the Gadarenes

A crowd soon gathered around Jesus, but they were frightened when they saw the man who had been demon possessed, for he was sitting there fully clothed and perfectly sane.

—Mark 5:15

DAY 15—A woman with internal bleeding

She had heard about Jesus, so she came up behind him through the crowd and touched the fringe of his robe. For she thought to herself, "If I can just touch his clothing, I will be healed." Immediately the bleeding stopped, and she could feel that she had been healed!

—Mark 5:27-28

DAY 16—A Galilean leper

Suddenly, a man with leprosy approached Jesus. He knelt before him, worshiping. "Lord," the man asked, "if you want to, you can make me well again." Jesus touched him. "I want to," he said. "Be healed!" And instantly the leprosy disappeared.

—Matthew 8:2-3

DAY 17—THE FATHER OF A DEMONIAC SON

The father instantly replied, "I do believe, but help me not to doubt!" When Jesus saw that the crowd of onlookers was growing, he rebuked the evil spirit. "Spirit of deafness and muteness," he said, "I command you to come out of this child and never enter him again!"...Jesus took him by the hand and helped him to his feet, and he stood up.

—MARK 9:24–25, 27

DAY 18—BLIND BARTIMAEUS

When Bartimaeus heard that Jesus from Nazareth was nearby, he began to shout out, "Jesus, Son of David, have mercy on me!"..."What do you want me to do for you?" Jesus asked. "Teacher," the blind man said, "I want to see!" And Jesus said to him, "Go your way. Your faith has healed you." And instantly the blind man could see!

—MARK 10:47, 51–52

DAY 19—A PARALYTIC

Some men came carrying a paralyzed man on a sleeping mat. They tried to push through the crowd to Jesus, but they couldn't reach him. So they went up to the roof, took off some tiles, and lowered the sick man down into the crowd, still on his mat, right in front of Jesus. Seeing their faith, Jesus said to the man, "Son, your sins are forgiven...Is it easier to say, 'Your sins are forgiven' or 'Get up and walk'? I will prove to you that I, the Son of Man, have the authority on earth to forgive sins." Then Jesus turned to the paralyzed man and said, "Stand up, take up your mat, and go on home, because you are healed!"

—LUKE 5:18–20, 23–24

DAY 20—AN IMMORAL WOMAN

A certain immoral woman heard he was there and brought a beautiful jar filled with expensive perfume. Then she knelt behind him at his feet, weeping. Her tears fell on his feet, and she wiped them off with her hair. Then she kept kissing his feet and putting perfume on them..."I tell you, her sins—and they are many—have been forgiven, so she has shown me much love. But a person who is forgiven little shows only little love." Then Jesus said to the woman, "Your sins are forgiven."

—LUKE 7:37–38, 47–48

DAY 21—A SAMARITAN LEPER

As he entered the village there, ten lepers stood at a distance, crying out, "Jesus, Master, have mercy on us!" He looked at them and said, "Go and show yourselves to the priests." And as they went, their leprosy disappeared. One of them, when he saw that he was healed, came back to Jesus, shouting, "Praise God, I'm healed!"

—LUKE 17:12–15

DAY 22—A TAX COLLECTOR

But the tax collector stood at a distance and dared not even lift his eyes to heaven as he prayed. Instead, he beat his chest in sorrow, saying, "O God, be merciful to me, for I am a sinner." I tell you, this sinner, not the Pharisee, returned home justified before God. For the proud will be humbled, but the humble will be honored.

—LUKE 18:13–14

DAY 23—ZACCHAEUS

Meanwhile, Zacchaeus stood there and said to the Lord, "I will give half my wealth to the poor, Lord, and if I have overcharged people on their taxes, I will give them back four times as much!" Jesus responded, "Salvation has come to this home today, for this man has shown himself to be a son of Abraham."

—LUKE 19:8–9

DAY 24—A WOMAN WITH AN EIGHTEEN-YEAR INFIRMITY

One Sabbath day as Jesus was teaching in a synagogue, he saw a woman who had been crippled by an evil spirit. She had been bent double for eighteen years and was unable to stand up straight. When Jesus saw her, he called her over and said, "Woman you are healed of your sickness!" Then he touched her, and instantly she could stand straight. How she praised and thanked God!

—LUKE 13:10–13

DAY 25—MARY MAGDALENE

It was early on Sunday morning when Jesus rose from the dead, and the first person who saw him was Mary Magdalene, the woman from whom he had cast out seven demons.

—MARK 16:9

DAY 26—The centurion at the cross

The Roman officer and the other soldiers at the cruci-
fixion were terrified by the earthquake and all that had
happened. They said, "Truly, this was the Son of God!"
                                              —*Matthew 27:54*

DAY 27—The thief on the cross

Then he said, "Jesus, remember me when you come
into your Kingdom." And Jesus replied, "I assure you,
today you will be with me in paradise."
                                              —*Luke 23:42-43*

DAY 28—Our Healer

And the Lord will protect you from all sickness. He will
not let you suffer from the terrible diseases you knew in
Egypt, but he will bring them all on your enemies.
                                              —*Deuteronomy 7:15*

DAY 29—Our Healer

Dear friend, I am praying that all is well with you and
that your body is as healthy as I know your soul is.
                                              —*3 John 2*

DAY 30—Our Healer

O Lord my God, I cried out to you for help, and you
restored my health.
                                              —*Psalm 30:2*[1]

Nutritional Regimen

Real Food Is Fabulous

Green Leafy and Cruciferous Vegetables

THIS IS WHERE THE POWER STARTS. Popeye was right. Think green. Experiment. Eat them raw in salads, lightly steam them, find new recipes that use them or juice them. Understand that they build health. They protect us from all diseases, including cancer. The chlorophyll in green foods helps revitalize every system in the body.

Especially include the following cruciferous vegetables:

- Cabbage (try all the colors and varieties)
- Broccoli
- Cauliflower
- Watercress
- Bok choy
- Radishes
- Rutabaga and turnips
- Kohlrabi, kale, mustard greens and collards (also leafy green vegetables)
- Brussels sprouts

The juice of green plants works quickly at the cellular level. Barley and wheat grass juices are widely available (always choose products made from organically grown cereal grasses). Enjoy adding these life-giving foods during the first month of your incredible journey.

Exercise Regimen

A Body I Can Live With!

Restoring His Temple

THE FOLLOWING EXERCISE REGIMEN IS A SCHEDULE of daily exercises that will enable you to restore and recondition your body—starting at any level. Please refer to detailed instructions and demonstration photos on page 221 to begin your regimen.

You will need to add to the charted strength and flexibility exercise regimen a consistent form of aerobic exercise as well. Perhaps you could choose a different form of aerobics for each month, such as walking, swimming, tennis, bicycling and others—or a combination of these. Twenty or thirty minutes of daily aerobic exercise will move you along your journey toward optimum health.

As you successfully complete your first month, you will want to follow the chart for each following month that increases your regimen appropriately. Please refer to demonstration photos on page 221 to begin your regimen.

IMPORTANT STRENGTH-TRAINING INSTRUCTIONS

Begin slowly, especially with the upper body exercises. We suggest 8 to 12 repetitions for each strength training exercise (except the push-ups). Rest after the first set. If you are able, do another set of repetitions. Rest again. If you are able, do a third set of repetitions.

Remember that it does not matter how few repetitions you are able to do in the beginning. Stay on schedule. You will gain strength every day. On the days you are not strength training, your muscles are repairing and growing stronger.

Gradually work up to the following schedule for each strength-training exercise (except push-ups):

First set:	8 to 12 repetitions Rest for one to two minutes
Second set:	8 to 12 repetitions Rest for one to two minutes
Third set:	8 to 12 repetitions Rest for one to two minutes

Strength training (Do each exercise on the days indicated)

EXERCISE	DAYS OF WEEK	1ST MONTH WEIGHTS
1. BICEPS (ARMS)	W	5–8 lb.
2. DELTOIDS (SHOULDERS)	W	3 lb.
3. ERECTOR SPINAE (BACK)	W	no ankle weight
4. TRICEPS (ARM)	W	one 8 lb.
5. PECS (CHEST)	W	5 lb.
6. ABS	M, W, F, Sa	no weights
7. PUSH-UPS	Sa	10 reps
8. SQUATS	M, F	no weights
9. OUTER THIGH	M, F	no weights
10. INNER THIGH	M, F	no weights

Flexibility training (Do each exercise on the days indicated)

EXERCISE	DAYS OF WEEK
1. STANDING LONG STRETCH (FULL BODY)	T, Th, Sa, Su
2. CALF STRETCH (LOWER BACK OF LEG)	T, Th, Sa, Su
3. HAMSTRING STRETCH (BACK OF THE THIGH, LOWER BACK, BUTTOCKS)	W, Th, Sa, Su
4. QUAD STRETCH (FRONT OF THE THIGH)	Th, Sa, Su
5. LONG STRETCH (FULL BODY)	M, T, Th, F, Sa, Su
6. OUTER THIGH (IT BAND)	M, T, Th, F, Sa, Su

7. BOW (BACK, GLUTEALS)	M, T, W, Th, F, Sa, Su
8. STATIC (LEGS AND BACK)	M, T, W, Th, F, Sa, Su
9. INNER THIGH	M, T, Th, F, Sa, Su
10. TRICEPS (UPPER BACK OF ARM)	M, T, W, Th, F, Sa, Su

Milestone Two

We Honor His Temple

We live and move and have our being in Christ, we know that our bodies are not our own, and we stand in awe of the truth that we have become the holy temple of the Lord, a part of the dwelling where God lives by His Spirit.

Vision

THE WORD OF GOD GIVES US A BLUEPRINT for constructing the most meaningful lifestyle change model—a model that facilitates the path to positive change by the power of His Spirit. In Christ, we grow confident in the outcome of our journey without comprehending the route, or what seem to be the detours. Failure isn't a destination; it's a wrong turn. Restoration and new awakenings await every contrite heart. We are already perfect in Him.

Spiritual Regimen

Living Each Hour in His Power

Second Month

Hearing His Voice and Obeying His Word

DAY 31

> The LORD nurses them when they are sick and eases their pain and discomfort.
>
> —*PSALM 41:3*

DAY 32

> Honor your father and mother. Then you will live a long, full life in the land the LORD your God will give you.
>
> —*EXODUS 20:12*

DAY 33

> My child, never forget the things I have taught you. Store my commands in your heart, for they will give you a long and satisfying life.
>
> —*PROVERBS 3:1-2*

DAY 34

> Don't lose sight of my words. Let them penetrate deep within your heart, for they bring life and radiant health to anyone who discovers their meaning.
>
> —*PROVERBS 4:21-22*

DAY 35

Jesus traveled throughout Galilee teaching in the synagogues, preaching everywhere the Good News about the Kingdom. And he healed people who had every kind of sickness and disease.

—Matthew **4:23**

DAY 36

Yes, ask anything in my name, and I will do it!

—John **14:14**

DAY 37

Are there any among you sick? They should call for the elders of the church and have them pray over them, anointing them with oil in the name of the Lord. And their prayer offered in faith will heal the sick, and the Lord will make them well.

—James **5:14–15**

DAY 38

But for you who fear my name, the Sun of Righteousness will rise with healing in his wings.

—Malachi **4:2**

DAY 39

Send your healing power; may miraculous signs and wonders be done through the name of your holy servant Jesus.

—Acts **4:30**

DAY 40

Listen to me! You can pray for anything, and if you believe, you will have it.

—Mark **11:24**

DAY 41

He was absolutely convinced that God was able to do anything he promised. And because of Abraham's faith, God declared him to be righteous.

—Romans **4:21–22**

DAY 42

I also tell you this: If two of you agree down here on earth concerning anything you ask, my Father in heaven will do it for you.

—Matthew **18:19**

DAY 43

Don't you realize that all of you together are the temple of God and that the Spirit of God lives in you? God will bring ruin on anyone who ruins his temple. For God's temple is holy, and you Christians are that temple.

—*1 Corinthians 3:16–17*

DAY 44

The Spirit of God, who raised Jesus from the dead, lives in you. And just as he raised Christ from the dead, he will give life to your mortal body by this same Spirit living within you.

—*Romans 8:11*

DAY 45

He spoke, and they were healed—snatched from the door of death.

—*Psalm 107:20*

DAY 46

So let us come boldly to the throne of our gracious God. There we will receive his mercy, and we will find grace to help us when we need it.

—*Hebrews 4:16*

DAY 47

The Lord will bless everything that you do and will fill your storehouses with grain. The Lord your God will bless you in the land he is giving you.

—*Deuteronomy 28:8*

DAY 48

For God is working in you, giving you the desire to obey him and the power to do what pleases him.

—*Philippians 2:13*

DAY 49

So, you see, it is impossible to please God without faith. Anyone who wants to come to him must believe that there is a God and that he rewards those who sincerely seek him.

—*Hebrews 11:6*

DAY 50

But you belong to God, my dear children. You have already won your fight with these false prophets, because the Spirit who lives in you is greater than the spirit who lives in the world.

—1 John 4:4

DAY 51

So humble yourselves before God. Resist the Devil, and he will flee from you.

—James 4:7

DAY 52

For every child of God defeats this evil world by trusting Christ to give the victory.

—1 John 5:4

DAY 53

For God has not given us a spirit of fear and timidity, but of power, love, and self-discipline.

—2 Timothy 1:7

DAY 54

Yet faith comes from listening to this message of good news—the Good News about Christ.

—Romans 10:17

DAY 55

Then Jesus said to the disciples, "Have faith in God."

—Mark 11:22

DAY 56

Fight the good fight for what we believe. Hold tightly to the eternal life that God has given you, which you have confessed so well before many witnesses.

—1 Timothy 6:12

DAY 57

What is faith? It is the confident assurance that what we hope for is going to happen. It is the evidence of things we cannot yet see.

—Hebrews 11:1

DAY 58

You haven't done this before. Ask, using my name, and you will receive, and you will have abundant joy.

—*John 16:24*

DAY 59

And no doubt you know that God anointed Jesus of Nazareth with the Holy Spirit and with power. Then Jesus went around doing good and healing all who were oppressed by the Devil, for God was with Him.

—*Acts 10:38*

DAY 60

He heals the brokenhearted, binding up their wounds.

—*Psalm 147:3*

Second Month

Real Food Is Fabulous

Essential Fatty Acids (EFAs)

THE SECOND CATEGORY OF POWER FOODS focuses on the omega-3 and omega-6 fatty acids.

- Friendly flaxseed: We need to be certain that we are getting omega-3 precursors every day. A main source for these is linolenic acid derived from freshly ground flaxseed.

- Cold-water fish: Adding salmon, sardines, mackerel, herring or trout to your diet several times a week will supply the needed omega-3 derivatives (EPA and DHA) as well.

- Soybeans: This inexpensive legume is a good source of omega-6 precursors.

- Important supplements: The omega-6 derivative, GLA, must be supplemented in your diet from borage, primrose or black currant oil. These vital nutrients are available as supplements in your favorite health food store.

- Most Americans already consume an abundance of omega-6 precursors in their diets from sunflower, safflower and corn oils.

A Body I Can Live With!

Restoring His Temple

P<small>LEASE</small> R<small>EFER</small> to detailed instructions and demonstration photos on page 221 to begin your regimen. Do not begin month two levels of exercise without first completing those for month one.

Remember, you are gradually working up to the following schedule for each strength-training exercise (except push-ups):

First set:	8 to 12 repetitions Rest for one to two minutes
Second set:	8 to 12 repetitions Rest for one to two minutes
Third set:	8 to 12 repetitions Rest for one to two minutes

Strength training (Do each exercise on the days indicated)

E<small>XERCISE</small>	D<small>AYS OF</small> W<small>EEK</small>	2<small>ND</small> M<small>ONTH</small> W<small>EIGHTS</small>
1. B<small>ICEPS</small> (A<small>RMS</small>)	W	8–10 lb.
2. D<small>ELTOIDS</small> (S<small>HOULDERS</small>)	W	3–5 lb.
3. E<small>RECTOR</small> S<small>PINAE</small> (B<small>ACK</small>)	W	1 lb. ankle weight <small>FLOOR POSITION</small>
4. T<small>RICEPS</small> (A<small>RM</small>)	W	one 10 lb.
5. P<small>ECS</small> (C<small>HEST</small>)	W	5 lb.

6. ABS	M, W, F, Sa	1 lb. ankle weight ON HIP LIFTS
7. PUSH-UPS	Sa	15 reps
8. SQUATS	M, F	two 5 lb. weights
9. OUTER THIGH	M, F	1 lb. ankle weight
10. INNER THIGH	M, F	1 lb. ankle weight

Flexibility training (Do each exercise on the days indicated)

EXERCISE	DAYS OF WEEK
1. STANDING LONG STRETCH (FULL BODY)	T, Th, Sa, Su
2. CALF STRETCH (LOWER BACK OF LEG)	T, Th, Sa, Su
3. HAMSTRING STRETCH (BACK OF THE THIGH, LOWER BACK, BUTTOCKS)	T, W, Th, Sa, Su
4. QUAD STRETCH (FRONT OF THE THIGH)	T, Th, Sa, Su
5. LONG STRETCH (FULL BODY)	M, T, Th, F, Sa, Su
6. OUTER THIGH (IT BAND)	M, T, Th, F, Sa, Su
7. BOW (BACK, GLUTEALS)	M, T, W, Th, F, Sa, Su
8. STATI (LEGS AND BACK)	M, T, W, Th, F, Sa, Su
9. INNER THIGH	M, T, Th, F, Sa, Su
10. TRICEPS (UPPER BACK OF ARM)	M, T, W, Th, F, Sa, Su

Milestone Three
We Celebrate His Provision

When we recognize our roles as stewards of the soil, air and water, and find in our hearts unspeakable gratitude to God for His provision of clothing, food and shelter, we are able to grasp the wonder and the fragility of life.

Vision

THROUGHOUT THE GOSPELS and the Pauline epistles, the Lord teaches us to be good and grateful stewards of our Father's world. God's love, discipline and mercy cause us to grow weary of our own ways and seek His peace.

When we find we are no longer able to celebrate the range and variety of whole foods (as He designed them), when we cannot recognize the worth of pure water, and when we no longer feel or express a profound gratitude for clothing and shelter—we cannot be fully alive in Him.

As we turn our attention to those in hunger and need, He rescues us from our barrenness and renews our lives by His Spirit. We must see our poverty in order to celebrate His provision.

Living Each Hour in His Power

The Names of Christ

DAY 61—ADVOCATE

My dear children, I am writing this to you so that you will not sin. But if you do sin, there is someone to plead for you before the Father. He is Jesus Christ, the one who pleases God completely.

—*1 JOHN 2:1*

DAY 62—ALMIGHTY

"I am the Alpha and the Omega—the beginning and the end," says the Lord God. "I am the one who is, who always was, and who is still to come, the Almighty One."

—*REVELATION 1:8*

DAY 63—AUTHOR

We do this by keeping our eyes on Jesus, on whom our faith depends from start to finish

—*HEBREWS 12:2*

DAY 64—BREAD OF LIFE

Jesus replied, "I am the bread of life. No one who comes to me will ever be hungry again. Those who believe in me will never thirst."

—*JOHN 6:35*

DAY 65—Counselor

For a child is born to us, a son is given to us. And the government will rest on his shoulders. These will be his royal titles: Wonderful Counselor, Mighty God, Everlasting Father, Prince of Peace.

—Isaiah 9:6

DAY 66—Deliverer

And so all Israel will be saved. Do you remember what the prophets said about this? "A Deliverer will come from Jerusalem, and he will turn Israel from the ungodliness. And then I will keep my covenant with them and take away their sins."

—Romans 11:26–27

DAY 67—Immanuel

Look! The virgin will conceive a child! She will give birth to a son, and he will be called Immanuel.

—Matthew 1:23

DAY 68—Eternal life

He is the only true God, and he is eternal life.

—1 John 5:20

DAY 69—Friend of sinners

And I, the Son of Man, feast and drink, and you say, "He's a glutton and a drunkard, and a friend of the worst sort of sinners!" But wisdom is shown to be right by what results from it.

—Matthew 11:19

DAY 70—High Priest

Therefore, it was necessary for Jesus to be in every respect like us, his brothers and sisters, so that he could be our merciful and faithful High Priest before God.

—Hebrews 2:17

DAY 71—Jehovah

Trust in the Lord always, for the Lord God is the eternal Rock.

—Isaiah 26:4

Third Month

DAY 72—LAMB OF GOD

The next day John saw Jesus coming toward him and he said, "Look! There is the Lamb of God who takes away the sin of the world."

—JOHN 1:29

DAY 73—LIVING BREAD

I am the living bread that came down out of heaven. Anyone who eats this bread will live forever; this bread is my flesh, offered so the world may live.

—JOHN 6:51

DAY 74—LORD OF LORDS

On his robe and thigh was written this title: King of kings and Lord of lords.

—REVELATION 19:16

DAY 75—MEDIATOR

For there is only one God and one Mediator who can reconcile God and people. He is the man Jesus Christ.

—1 TIMOTHY 2:5

DAY 76—REFINER

He will sit and judge like a refiner of silver, watching closely as the dross is burned away.

—MALACHI 3:3

DAY 77—REFUGE

But to the poor, O LORD, you are a refuge from the storm. To the needy in distress, you are a shelter from the rain and the heat.

—ISAIAH 25:4

DAY 78—ROCK

They made light of the Rock of their salvation.

—DEUTERONOMY 32:15

DAY 79—SERVANT

Look at my servant, whom I strengthen. He is my chosen one, and I am pleased with him. I have put my spirit upon him. He will reveal justice to the nations.

—ISAIAH 42:1

DAY 80—SHEPHERD

The LORD is my shepherd; I have everything I need.

—PSALM 23:1

DAY 81—SON OF DAVID

He was in the center of the procession, and the crowds all around him were shouting, "Praise God for the Son of David! Bless the one who comes in the name of the Lord! Praise God in the highest heaven!"

—MATTHEW 21:9

DAY 82—SON OF MAN

"I will prove that I, the Son of Man, have the authority on earth to forgive sins." Then Jesus turned to the paralyzed man and said, "Stand up, take up your mat, and go on home, because you are healed!"

—MATTHEW 9:6

DAY 83—SON OF ABRAHAM

This is a record of the ancestors of Jesus the Messiah, a descendant of King David and of Abraham.

—MATTHEW 1:1

DAY 84—SON OF THE HIGHEST

He will be very great and will be called the Son of the Most High. And the Lord God will give him the throne of his ancestor David.

—LUKE 1:32

DAY 85—STONE

Then Jesus asked them, "Didn't you ever read this in the Scriptures? 'The stone rejected by the builders has now become the chief cornerstone. This is the Lord's doing, and it is marvelous to see.'

—MATTHEW 21:42

DAY 86—SUN OF RIGHTEOUSNESS

But for you who fear my name, the Sun of Righteousness will rise with healing in his wings. And you will go free, leaping with joy like calves let out to pasture.

—MALACHI 4:2

DAY 87—TEACHER

"As you go into the city," he told them, "you will see a certain man. Tell him, 'The Teacher says, My time has come, and I will eat the Passover meal with my disciples at your house.'"

—MATTHEW 26:18

DAY 88—WONDERFUL

For a child is born to us, a son is given to us. And the government will rest on his shoulders. These will be his royal titles: Wonderful Counselor, Mighty God, Everlasting Father, Prince of Peace.

—ISAIAH 9:6

DAY 89—WORD

In the beginning the Word already existed. He was with God, and he was God.

—JOHN 1:1

DAY 90—MESSIAH

Now listen and understand! Seven sets of seven plus sixty-two sets of seven will pass from the time the command is given to rebuild Jerusalem until the Anointed One comes.

—DANIEL 9:25[2]

Real Food Is Fabulous

Phytoestrogens and Legumes

THE TWO MAJOR PHYTOESTROGEN groups are:

- Isoflavones, which are found in the greatest concentration in soybeans (a legume)

- Lignans, which are found in the greatest concentration in flaxseed

The benefits of isoflavones (from soybeans) and lignans (from flaxseed) give us every reason to include soybeans and flaxseed in the daily dietary regimen. They are crucial in:

- Preventing heart disease, cancer and osteoporosis
- Detoxifying our bodies
- Restoring cell membrane function
- Blood sugar regulation
- Enzyme modulation
- Weight management
- Overcoming hypocholesterolemia
- Overcoming hypolipidemia

For those who are concerned about the digestive problems associated with soybeans in particular, and beans in general, you will be helped greatly by taking a premium digestive enzyme supplement with your meal of legumes.

You will want to discover healthy recipes that use a variety of legumes, especially concentrating on the following:

- Soybeans
- Pinto beans
- Lentils

A dietary regimen that features legumes offers many important benefits:

- Lower cholesterol levels
- Improvement in glucose tolerance
- Improvement in glucose control for diabetics
- Reduction in the risk of breast cancer

A Body I Can Live With!

Restoring His Temple

Do NOT PROCEED TO THIS LEVEL OF EXERCISE WITHOUT first completing the suggested regimen for months one and two. If you have done that, you are ready to reach the midway point of your 180-day journey of fitness through exercise. Please refer to detailed instructions and demonstration photos on page 221 to begin your regimen. Enjoy the journey!

Remember, you are gradually working up to the following schedule for each strength-training exercise (except push-ups):

First set:	8 to 12 repetitions
	Rest for one to two minutes
Second set:	8 to 12 repetitions
	Rest for one to two minutes
Third set:	8 to 12 repetitions
	Rest for one to two minutes

Strength training (Do each exercise on the days indicated)

EXERCISE	DAYS OF WEEK	3RD MONTH WEIGHTS
1. BICEPS (ARMS)	W	10 lb.
2. DELTOIDS (SHOULDERS)	W	5 lb.
3. ERECTOR SPINAE (BACK)	W	1½ lb. ankle weight HANDS & KNEES POSITION
4. TRICEPS (ARM)	W	one 10 lb.

5. PECS (CHEST)	W	8 lb.
6. ABS	M, W, F, Sa	1½ lb. HOLD HIPS UP FOR 3 COUNTS
7. PUSH-UPS	Sa	15 reps
8. SQUATS	M, F	two 5 lb. weights
9. OUTER THIGH	M, F	1½ lb. ankle weights
10. INNER THIGH	M, F	1½ lb. ankle weights

Flexibility training (Do each exercise on the days indicated)

EXERCISE	DAYS OF WEEK
1. STANDING LONG STRETCH (FULL BODY)	T, Th, Sa, Su
2. CALF STRETCH (LOWER BACK OF LEG)	T, Th, Sa, Su
3. HAMSTRING STRETCH (BACK OF THE THIGH, LOWER BACK, BUTTOCKS)	T, W, Th, Sa, Su
4. QUAD STRETCH (FRONT OF THE THIGH)	T, Th, Sa, Su
5. LONG STRETCH (FULL BODY)	M, T, Th, F, Sa, Su
6. OUTER THIGH (IT BAND)	M, T, Th, F, Sa, Su
7. BOW (BACK, GLUTEALS)	M, T, W, Th, F, Sa, Su
8. STATIC (LEGS AND BACK)	M, T, W, Th, F, Sa, Su
9. INNER THIGH	M, T, Th, F, Sa, Su
10. TRICEPS (UPPER BACK OF ARM)	M, T, W, Th, F, Sa, Su

Third Month

Milestone Four

We Walk in His Power

The revelation of His resurrection gives us victory over sin and death and enables us to move in the same power that raised Jesus from the dead.

Vision

THE CORE OF OUR FAITH, and the only hope for finding meaning in life, is the truth that Jesus Christ arose from the dead! He lives, and we can know Him! This certainty causes us to seek His face when we are confounded by the darkest trial or annoyed by the slightest inconvenience. That resurrection power enables us to find the will and wisdom to make vital changes in our lives.

Living Each Hour in His Power

We Learn to Trust Him

DAY 91

What is faith? It is the confident assurance that what we hope for is going to happen. It is the evidence of things we cannot yet see.

—HEBREWS *11:1*

DAY 92

Now stand here and see the great thing the LORD is about to do.

—*1 SAMUEL 12:16*

DAY 93

The LORD is my light and my salvation—so why should I be afraid? The LORD protects me from danger—so why should I tremble?

—PSALM *27:1*

DAY 94

It is better to trust the LORD than to put confidence in people.

—PSALM *118:8*

DAY 95

The strength of a horse does not impress him; how puny in his sight is the strength of a man. Rather, the LORD's delight is in those who honor him, those who put their hope in his unfailing love.

—PSALM *147:10–11*

Fourth Month

DAY 96

Trust in the LORD with all your heart; do not depend on your own understanding. Seek his will in all you do, and he will direct your paths.

—PROVERBS 3:5–6

DAY 97

True humility and fear of the LORD lead to riches, honor, and long life.

—PROVERBS 22:4

DAY 98

You will keep in perfect peace all who trust in you, whose thoughts are fixed on you!

—ISAIAH 26:3

DAY 99

Suddenly, a man with leprosy approached Jesus. He knelt before him, worshiping. "Lord," the man asked, "if you want to, you can make me well again." Jesus touched him. "I want to," he said. "Be healed!" And instantly the leprosy disappeared.

—MATTHEW 8:2–3

DAY 100

"You didn't have enough faith," Jesus told them. "I assure you, even if you had faith as small as a mustard seed you could say to this mountain, 'Move from here to there,' and it would move. Nothing would be impossible."

—MATTHEW 17:20

DAY 101

Then Jesus told them, "I assure you, if you have faith and don't doubt, you can do things like this and much more. You can even say to this mountain, 'May God lift you up and throw you into the sea,' and it will happen. If you believe, you will receive whatever you ask for in prayer."

—MATTHEW 21:21–22

DAY 102

"What do you mean, 'If I can'?" Jesus asked. "Anything is possible if a person believes."

—MARK 9:23

Fourth Month

DAY 103

He said to them, "Let the children come to me. Don't stop them! For the Kingdom of God belongs to such as these. I assure you, anyone who doesn't have their kind of faith will never get into the Kingdom of God." Then he took the children into his arms and placed his hands on their heads and blessed them.

—MARK 10:14–16

DAY 104

Listen to me! You can pray for anything, and if you believe, you will have it.

—MARK 11:24

DAY 105

This Good News tells us how God makes us right in His sight. This is accomplished from start to finish by faith. As the Scriptures say, "It is through faith that a righteous person has life."

—ROMANS 1:17

DAY 106

And a righteous person will live by faith. But I will have no pleasure in anyone who turns away. But we are not like those who turn their backs on God and seal their fate. We have faith that assures our salvation.

—HEBREWS 10:38–39

DAY 107

Abraham never wavered in believing God's promise. In fact, his faith grew stronger, and in this he brought glory to God.

—ROMANS 4:20

DAY 108

So we don't look at the troubles we can see right now; rather, we look forward to what we have not yet seen. For the troubles we see will soon be over, but the joys to come will last forever.

—2 CORINTHIANS 4:18

DAY 109

But when you ask him, be sure that you really expect him to answer, for a doubtful mind is as unsettled as a wave of the sea that is driven and tossed by the wind.

—JAMES 1:6

DAY 110

And God, in his mighty power, will protect you until you receive this salvation, because you are trusting him. It will be revealed on the last day for all to see. So be truly glad! There is wonderful joy ahead, even though it is necessary for you to endure many trials for a while.

—1 Peter 1:5-6

DAY 111

For every child of God defeats this evil world by trusting Christ to give the victory. And the ones who win this battle against the world are the ones who believe that Jesus is the Son of God.

—1 John 5:4-5

DAY 112

Accept Christians who are weak in faith, and don't argue with them about what they think is right or wrong.

—Romans 14:1

DAY 113

Be on guard. Stand true to what you believe. Be courageous. Be strong.

—1 Corinthians 16:13

DAY 114

Examine yourselves to see if your faith is really genuine. Test yourselves. If you cannot tell that Jesus Christ is among you, it means you have failed the test.

—2 Corinthians 13:5

DAY 115

The name of Jesus has healed this man—and you know how lame he was before. Faith in Jesus' name has caused this healing before your very eyes.

—Acts 3:16

DAY 116

Jesus turned around and said to her, "Daughter, be encouraged! Your faith has made you well." And the woman was healed at that moment.

—Matthew 9:22

DAY 117

Let me say first of all that your faith in God is becoming known throughout the world. How I thank God through Jesus Christ for each one of you.

—ROMANS 1:8

DAY 118

I always thank God when I pray for you, Philemon, because I keep hearing of your trust in the Lord Jesus and your love for all of God's people.

—PHILEMON 4–5

DAY 119

If I had the gift of prophecy, and if I knew all the mysteries of the future and knew everything about everything, but didn't love others, what good would I be? And if I had the gift of faith so that I could speak to a mountain and make it move, without love I would be no good to anybody.

—1 CORINTHIANS 13:2

DAY 120

There is only one Lord, one faith, one baptism.

—EPHESIANS 4:5

Real Food Is Fabulous

Nourish Your Body With Phytochemicals

PHYTOCHEMICALS ARE NONNUTRITIVE PLANT CHEMICALS that contain protective, disease-preventing compounds. As we consider the important roles that fruits and grains play in our diet, we need to be mindful of our personal challenges regarding glucose intolerance, insulin resistance, allergies and other chronic conditions outlined in Part Three. These conditions will dictate our approach to introducing the foods listed in the chart below. Choose those foods that you can presently tolerate, and then, as your health improves, experiment with introducing others.

The chart below gives you some suggestions for eating whole foods that provide healing phytochemicals.[3] You will note that some foods listed are among those you have already begun to add into your diet, such as the cruciferous vegetables.

MOST COMMONLY STUDIED PHYTOCHEMICALS	
FOOD	PHYTOCHEMICAL(S)
Allium vegetables (garlic, onions, chives, leeks)	Allyl sulfides

Cruciferous vegetables (broccoli, cauliflower, cabbage, Brussels sprouts, kale, turnips, bok choy, kohlrabi)	Indoles/glucosinolates Sulfaforaphane Isothiocyanates/ thiocyanates Thiols
Solanaceous vegetables (tomatoes, peppers)	Lycopene
Umbelliferous vegetables (carrots, celery, cilantro, parsley, parsnips)	Carotenoids Phthalides Polyacetylenes
Compositae plants (artichoke)	Silymarin
Citrus fruits (oranges, lemons, grapefruit) Glucarates	Monoterpenes (limonene) Carotenoids
Other fruits (grapes, berries, cherries, apples, cantaloupe, watermelon, pomegranate)	Ellagic acid Phenols, Flavonoids (quercetin)
Beans, grains, seeds (soybeans, oats, barley, brown rice, whole wheat, flaxseed) Protease inhibitors	Flavonoids (isoflavones) Phytic acid Saponins
Herbs, spices (ginger, mint, rosemary, thyme, oregano, sage, basil, tumeric, caraway, fennel)	Gingerols Flavonoids Monoterpenes (limonene)
Licorice root Green tea, Polyphenols	Glycyrrhizin Catechins

A Body I Can Live With!

Restoring His Temple

DO NOT PROCEED TO THIS LEVEL OF EXERCISE WITHOUT first completing the suggested regimen for previous months. Please refer to detailed instructions and demonstration photos on page 221 to begin your regimen.

Remember, you are gradually working up to the following schedule for each strength-training exercise (except push-ups):

First set: 8 to 12 repetitions
Rest for one to two minutes

Second set: 8 to 12 repetitions
Rest for one to two minutes

Third set: 8 to 12 repetitions
Rest for one to two minutes

Strength training (Do each exercise on the days indicated)

EXERCISE	DAYS OF WEEK	4TH MONTH WEIGHTS
1. BICEPS (ARMS)	W	10+ lb.
2. DELTOIDS (SHOULDERS)	W	5 lb.
3. ERECTOR SPINAE (BACK)	W	1½ lb. ankle weight HANDS & KNEES POSITION
4. TRICEPS (ARM)	W	one 15 lb. Body bar

Fourth Month

5. Pecs (Chest)	W	8 lb.
6. Abs	M, W, F, Sa	1½ lb. ankle weight
7. Push-ups	Sa	20 reps
8. Squats	M, F	one 15 lb. Body bar
9. Outer Thigh	M, F	1½ lb. ankle weight
10. Inner Thigh	M, F	1½ lb. ankle weight

Flexibility training (Do each exercise on the days indicated)

Exercise	Days of Week
1. Standing Long Stretch (Full body)	T, Th, Sa, Su
2. Calf Stretch (Lower back of leg)	T, Th, Sa, Su
3. Hamstring Stretch (Back of the thigh, lower back, buttocks)	T, W, Th, Sa, Su
4. Quad Stretch (Front of the thigh)	T, Th, Sa, Su
5. Long Stretch (Full body)	M, T, Th, F, Sa, Su
6. Outer Thigh (IT band)	M, T, Th, F, Sa, Su
7. Bow (Back, gluteals)	M, T, W, Th, F, Sa, Su
8. Static (Legs and back)	M, T, W, Th, F, Sa, Su
9. Inner Thigh	M, T, Th, F, Sa, Su
10. Triceps (Upper back of arm)	M, T, W, Th, F, Sa, Su

Fourth Month

Milestone Five

We Grow in His Wisdom

---

*As we hear His voice, we begin to imitate Christ in
our thoughts, words and actions.*

Vision

GROWING IN GODLY WISDOM doesn't come from
simply reading His Word or hearing the Word, but by
meditating on the Word until His thoughts become
our thoughts. We have an incredible account of the life
and death, words and actions of Christ. For those who
have ears to hear, He speaks through the Word—from
Genesis to Revelation.

He answers those who pray with His peace and His
power. Happiness and life are available to those who
embrace wisdom. How do we find wisdom? James,
Jesus' brother, tells us that we are to ask Him. If we
want to know what God wants us to do, we have only
to ask Him and He will tell us. We are to expect an
answer.

Living Each Hour in His Power

The Peace of God

DAY 121

> When he woke up, he rebuked the wind and said to the water, "Quiet down!" Suddenly the wind stopped, and there was a great calm.
>
> —MARK *4:39*

DAY 122

> May the LORD show you his favor and give you his peace.
>
> —NUMBERS *6:26*

DAY 123

> As for me, I am for peace; but when I speak, they are for war!
>
> —PSALM *120:7*

DAY 124

> Deceit fills hearts that are plotting evil; joy fills hearts that are planning peace!
>
> —PROVERBS *12:20*

DAY 125

> When the ways of people please the LORD, he makes even their enemies live at peace with them.
>
> —PROVERBS *16:7*

Fifth Month

DAY 126

A time to love and a time to hate. A time for war and a time for peace.

—*Ecclesiastes* **3:8**

DAY 127

Lord, you will grant us peace, for all we have accomplished is really from you.

—*Isaiah* **26:12**

DAY 128

How beautiful on the mountains are the feet of those who bring good news of peace and salvation, the news that the God of Israel reigns!

—*Isaiah* **52:7**

DAY 129

You will live in joy and peace. The mountains and hills will burst into song, and the trees of the field will clap their hands!

—*Isaiah* **55:12**

DAY 130

"Peace and prosperity will overflow Jerusalem like a river," says the Lord.

—*Isaiah* **66:12**

DAY 131

Salt is good for seasoning. But if it loses its flavor, how do you make it salty again? You must have the qualities of salt among yourselves and live in peace with each other.

—*Mark* **9:50**

DAY 132

We can rejoice, too, when we run into problems and trials, for we know that they are good for us—they help us learn to endure. And endurance develops strength of character in us, and character strengthens our confident expectation of salvation.

—*Romans* **5:3–4**

Fifth Month

DAY 133

For Christ himself has made peace between us Jews
and you Gentiles by making us all one people He has
broken down the wall of hostility that used to separate
us.

—EPHESIANS *2:14*

DAY 134

These trials are only to test your faith, to show that it is
strong and pure. It is being tested as fire tests and puri-
fies gold—and your faith is far more precious to God
than mere gold. So if your faith remains strong after
being tried by fiery trials, it will bring you much praise
and glory and honor on the day when Jesus Christ is
revealed to the whole world.

—*1 PETER 1:7*

DAY 135

Dear friends, don't be surprised at the fiery trials you
are going through, as if something strange were happening to you.

—*1 PETER 4:12*

DAY 136

Tears of joy will stream down their faces, and I will lead
them home with great care. They will walk beside quiet
streams and not stumble. For I am Israel's father, and
Ephraim is my oldest son.

—*JEREMIAH 31:9*

DAY 137

But even if my life is to be poured out like a drink
offering to complete the sacrifice of your faithful service
(that is, if I am to die for you), I will rejoice, and I want
to share my joy with all of you.

—*PHILIPPIANS 2:17*

DAY 138

So now we can rejoice in our wonderful new relationship with God—all because of what our Lord Jesus
Christ has done for us in making us friends of God.

—*ROMANS 5:11*

Fifth Month

DAY 139

But let all who take refuge in you rejoice; let them sing joyful praises forever. Protect them, so all who love your name may be filled with joy.

—Psalm 5:11

DAY 140

You love him even though you have never seen him. Though you do not see him, you trust him; and even now you are happy with a glorious, inexpressible joy.

—1 Peter 1:8

DAY 141

How we thank God for you! Because of you we have great joy in the presence of God.

—1 Thessalonians 3:9

DAY 142

I long to see you again, for I remember your tears as we parted. And I will be filled with joy when we are together again.

—2 Timothy 1:4

DAY 143

For the Kingdom of God is not a matter of what we eat or drink, but of living a life of goodness and peace and joy in the Holy Spirit.

—Romans 14:17

DAY 144

You have shown me the way of life, and you will give me wonderful joy in your presence.

—Acts 2:28

DAY 145

Light shines on the godly, and joy on those who do right.

—Psalm 97:11

DAY 146

And zealous? Yes, in fact, I harshly persecuted the church. And I obeyed the Jewish law so carefully that I was never accused of any fault.

—Philippians 3:6

Fifth Month

DAY 147

You will keep in perfect peace all who trust in you, whose thoughts are fixed on you!

—Isaiah **26:3**

DAY 148

If you do this, you will experience God's peace, which is far more wonderful than the human mind can understand. His peace will guard your hearts and minds as you live in Christ Jesus.

—Philippians **4:7**

DAY 149

But when the Holy Spirit controls our lives, he will produce this kind of fruit in us; love, joy, peace, patience, kindness, goodness, faithfulness, gentleness, and self-control. Here there is no conflict with the law.

—Galatians **5:22–23**

DAY 150

And all the people returned with Solomon to Jerusalem, playing flutes and shouting for joy. The celebration was so joyous and noisy that the earth shook with the sound.

—1 Kings **1:40**

Real Food Is Fabulous

Learning the Value of Complex Carbohydrates

COMPLEX CARBOHYDRATES ARE ALMOST ENTIRELY RECEIVED from plant foods. They include:

- Minimally processed grains
- Potatoes
- Beans
- Breads and pastas derived from the above

UNDERSTANDING INTACT GRAINS

Intact grains are grains that have not been milled or flaked. Both intact grains and flour products made from freshly milled flour containing all three parts of the kernel (germ, endosperm and bran) are truly whole grains. The wheat kernel (wheat berry) is the actual seed from which the wheat plant grows.

Most traditional supermarkets sell breads and cereal products marked "whole grain" that are not whole-grain products at all. The germ has been removed from these products to assure a long shelf life, thus increasing profits. The fact that real bread is not widely available to all families in America has contributed greatly to deficiencies in essential fatty acids, affecting over 80 percent of Americans.

Here is what we lose during the commercial milling process, and what remains:

- The germ that is removed is the embryo of the seed that comprises about 2.5 percent of the kernel weight and contains the greatest share of the B-complex vitamins, trace minerals and, most important, essential fatty acids. By removing the germ, the flour is devitalized.

- The bran is removed during the commercial milling of flour used for most breads, baked goods, cereals, etc. The bran contains important nutrients including indigestible cellulose material (fiber!), trace minerals, significant quantities of B-complex vitamins and a small amount of protein. The bran comprises about 14.5 percent of the kernel weight.

- The endosperm contains the greatest share of protein in the wheat kernel, as well as carbohydrates, iron and small amounts of B-complex vitamins such as riboflavin, niacin and thiamine. The endosperm is the part of the kernel retained as flour after the commercial milling process and comprises about 83 percent of the kernel weight.

Breads and baked goods using "freshly milled flour," containing all three parts of the kernel, are widely available in whole-foods supermarkets and health food stores around the country. These are truly life-giving products.

I RECOMMEND...

I recommend eating intact grains for optimal health. For those who want to make whole-grain breads, waffles, pancakes, muffins and other delightful products, a home flourmill is a must. These appliances are easy for us to operate, to clean and to store. We can add flaxseed, soy powder and beneficial ingredients to our whole-grain baked goods.

Experiment with your favorite recipes by substituting refined flour products for whole wheat and other intact grains to create delicious meals, whole-grain breads, waffles, pancakes, muffins and whole-grain pastas.

For anyone who is overweight, suffering from glucose intolerance or insulin resistance, the high-protein, high-fiber benefits of quinoa and buckwheat are important. For those who are more flexible, the world of milling and baking is a blessing.

Fifth Month

A Body I Can Live With!

Restoring His Temple

DO NOT PROCEED TO THIS LEVEL OF EXERCISE WITHOUT first completing the suggested regimen for previous months. Please refer to detailed instructions and demonstration photos on page 221 to begin your regimen. If you have arrived at this level, let me congratulate you on a job well done. You must be feeling great!

Remember, you are gradually working up to the following schedule for each strength-training exercise (except push-ups):

First set:	8 to 12 repetitions
	Rest for one to two minutes
Second set:	8 to 12 repetitions
	Rest for one to two minutes
Third set:	8 to 12 repetitions
	Rest for one to two minutes

Strength training (Do each exercise on the days indicated)

EXERCISE	DAYS OF WEEK	5TH MONTH WEIGHTS
1. BICEPS (ARMS)	W	12 lb.
2. DELTOIDS (SHOULDERS)	W	5 lb.
3. ERECTOR SPINAE (BACK)	W	2 lb. ankle weight HANDS & KNEES POSITION
4. TRICEPS (ARM)	W	one 15 lb. body bar

Fifth Month

209

5. PECS (CHEST)	W	8–10 lb.
6. ABS	M, W, F, Sa	2 lb. ankle weights
7. PUSH-UPS	Sa	25 reps
8. SQUATS	M, F	one 15–18 lb. body bar
9. OUTER THIGH	M, F	2 lb. ankle weight
10. INNER THIGH	M, F	2 lb. ankle weight

Flexibility training (Do each exercise on the days indicated)

EXERCISE	DAYS OF WEEK
1. STANDING LONG STRETCH (FULL BODY)	T, Th, Sa, Su
2. CALF STRETCH (LOWER BACK OF LEG)	T, Th, Sa, Su
3. HAMSTRING STRETCH (BACK OF THE THIGH, LOWER BACK, BUTTOCKS)	T, W, Th, Sa, Su
4. QUAD STRETCH (FRONT OF THE THIGH)	T, Th, Sa, Su
5. LONG STRETCH (FULL BODY)	M, T, Th, F, Sa, Su
6. OUTER THIGH (IT BAND)	M, T, Th, F, Sa, Su
7. BOW (BACK, GLUTEALS)	M, T, W, Th, F, Sa, Su
8. STATIC (LEGS AND BACK)	M, T, W, Th, F, Sa, Su
9. INNER THIGH	M, T, Th, F, Sa, Su
10. TRICEPS (UPPER BACK OF ARM)	M, T, W, Th, F, Sa, Su

Fifth Month

Milestone Six

We Walk in Freedom

When we receive God's love, joy, mercy, faith and forgiveness, we are able to embrace His calling on our lives!

Vision

THE APOSTLE PAUL TEACHES US that whatever we choose to obey becomes our master. If we are free from the power of sin, we choose holiness. Sin and holiness are not welcome words when we cling to a materialistic world. Many in our culture declare that sin and holiness are concepts consigned to a medieval world that is bound by ignorance and superstition. The truth is that scientism and unbelief enslave us and blind us to worlds of knowledge. Trapped in the darkness of the material world, we can neither embrace nor recognize God as the Creator of a universe that should fill us with reverence for Him.

By the power of the Holy Spirit, we overcome sin in our lives. We acknowledge our sin, we repent and we overcome the power of darkness. Freedom in Christ is available to those who call on His name and who believe that He arose from the dead. Those who know Him may rest assured that there is now no condemnation for those who belong to Christ Jesus! The same power that raised Christ from the dead frees us from the power of sin.

Spiritual Regimen

Living Each Hour in His Power

Empowered by the Holy Spirit

DAY 151

God alone made it possible for you to be in Christ Jesus. For our benefit God made Christ to be wisdom itself. He is the one who made us acceptable to God.

—*1 Corinthians 1:30*

DAY 152

For the Kingdom of God is not just fancy talk; it is living by God's power.

—*1 Corinthians 4:20*

DAY 153

But now your sins have been washed away, and you have been set apart for God. You have been made right with God because of what the Lord Jesus Christ and the Spirit of our God have done for you.

—*1 Corinthians 6:11*

DAY 154

But we know that there is only one God, the Father, who created everything, and we exist for him. And there is only one Lord, Jesus Christ, through whom God made everything and through whom we have been given life.

—*1 Corinthians 8:6*

DAY 155

Whatever you eat or drink or whatever you do, you must do all for the glory of God.

—*1 Corinthians 10:31*

DAY 156

Love is patient and kind. Love is not jealous or boastful or proud or rude. Love does not demand its own way. Love is not irritable, and it keeps no record of when it has been wronged.

—*1 Corinthians 13:4-5*

DAY 157

I have been crucified with Christ. I myself no longer live, but Christ lives in me. So I live my life in this earthly body by trusting in the Son of God, who loved me and gave himself for me.

—*Galatians 2:19-20*

DAY 158

All Scripture is inspired by God and is useful to teach us what is true and to make us realize what is wrong in our lives. It straightens us out and teaches us to do what is right.

—*2 Timothy 3:16*

DAY 159

Share each other's troubles and problems, and in this way obey the law of Christ.

—*Galatians 6:2*

DAY 160

And now you also have heard the truth, the Good News that God saves you. And when you believed in Christ, he identified you as his own by giving you the Holy Spirit, whom he promised long ago.

—*Ephesians 1:13*

DAY 161

The Spirit is God's guarantee that he will give us every-thing he promised and that he has purchased us to be his own people.

—*Ephesians 1:14*

Sixth Month

213

DAY 162

For we are God's masterpiece. He has created us anew in Christ Jesus, so that we can do the good things he planned for us long ago.

—*Ephesians 2:10*

DAY 163

I pray that from his glorious, unlimited resources he will give you mighty inner strength through his Holy Spirit.

—*Ephesians 3:16*

DAY 164

May you experience the love of Christ, though it is so great you will never fully understand it. Then you will be filled with the fullness of life and power that comes from God.

—*Ephesians 3:19*

DAY 165

By his mighty power at work within us, he is able to accomplish infinitely more than we would ever dare to ask or hope.

—*Ephesians 3:20*

DAY 166

Pray at all times and on every occasion in the power of the Holy Spirit. Stay alert and be persistent in your prayers for all Christians everywhere.

—*Ephesians 6:18*

DAY 167

Always be full of joy in the Lord. I say it again—rejoice!

—*Philippians 4:4*

DAY 168

We put no confidence in human effort. Instead, we boast about what Christ Jesus has done for us.

—*Philippians 3:3*

DAY 169

Confess your sins to each other and pray for each other so that you may be healed. The earnest prayer of a righteous person has great power and wonderful results.

—*James 5:16*

DAY 170

If you try to keep your life for yourself, you will lose it. But if you give up your life for me, you will find true life.

—*Luke 9:24*

DAY 171

God did not send his Son into the world to condemn it, but to save it.

—*John 3:17*

DAY 172

But the time is coming and is already here when true worshipers will worship the Father in spirit and in truth. The Father is looking for anyone who will worship him that way.

—*John 4:23*

DAY 173

If you are thirsty, come to me! If you believe in me, come and drink! For the Scriptures declare that rivers of living water will flow out from within.

—*John 7:37–38*

DAY 174

I am the light of the world. If you follow me, you won't be stumbling through the darkness, because you will have the light that leads to life.

—*John 8:12*

DAY 175

And this is the way to have eternal life—to know you, the only true God, and Jesus Christ, the one you sent to earth.

—*John 17:3*

DAY 176

We are made right in God's sight when we trust in Jesus Christ to take away our sins. And we all can be saved in this same way, no matter who we are or what we have done.

—*Romans 3:22*

Sixth Month

DAY 177

But God showed his great love for us by sending Christ to die for us while we were still sinners. And since we have been made right in God's sight by the blood of Christ, he will certainly save us from God's judgment.

—ROMANS *5:8–9*

DAY 178

The Spirit of God, who raised Jesus from the dead, lives in you. And just as he raised Christ from the dead, he will give life to your mortal body by this same Spirit living within you.

—ROMANS *8:11*

DAY 179

And we know that God causes everything to work together for the good of those who love God and are called according to his purpose for them.

—ROMANS *8:28*

DAY 180

Salvation that comes from trusting Christ—which is the message we preach—is already within easy reach. In fact, the Scriptures say, "The message is close at hand; it is on your lips and in your heart." For if you confess with your mouth that Jesus is Lord and believe in your heart that God raised him from the dead, you will be saved. For it is by believing in your heart that you are made right with God, and it is by confessing with your mouth that you are saved. As the Scriptures tell us, "Anyone who believes in him will not be disappointed." Jew and Gentile are the same in this respect. They all have the same Lord, who generously gives his riches to all who ask for them. For "Anyone who calls on the name of the Lord will be saved."

—ROMANS *10:8–13*

Real Food Is Fabulous

Healthy Choices for Animal Products

A PRIMARILY PLANT-BASED DIET IS NOT FOR EVERYONE. Some will still feel the need for the animal protein they have grown accustomed to eating throughout life. In that case, in order to ensure your journey toward optimal health, I would strongly suggest that you make every effort to make healthy choices according to the following considerations:

- Organic grass-fed beef is high in essential fatty acids; grain-fed beef is high in saturated fat. Choose beef that is grass fed, organically grown and has not been injected with hormones.

- Choose dairy products and that are certified organic, free from pesticides and hormones.

- Eggs should be from free-range chickens, free of hormones and antibiotics. Omega-3 eggs are a great source of fatty acids for those who choose to consume eggs. Commercial hens spend their entire lives in cages, ingesting chemicals and antibiotics. "Free-range" chickens roam freely, eating bugs, worms, etc. These hens and their eggs are free from antibiotics and chemicals.

- Consume chicken and turkey that are free range, free from antibiotics and hormones.

- Count the amount of saturated fat. If you suffer from

Sixth Month

217

chronic degenerative disease, extra-virgin olive oil (monounsaturated fat) and the essential fatty acids offer enormous health benefits; they also provide the fats we all need.

- We need adequate, not excessive, amounts of protein. Our level of activity determines the amount of protein that we need.

- If you are not a vegan, cultivate a taste for cold-water fish—salmon, sardines, mackerel, herring and trout. Recipes abound.

A Body I Can Live With!

Restoring His Temple

CONGRATULATIONS! It is not a simple achievement to arrive at month six of this regimen—congratulate yourself for a job well done! By now, you are probably understanding why it takes 180 days to establish lifestyle changes. Don't quit now—maintenance will keep you on track toward optimal health.

Do not proceed to this level of exercise without first completing the suggested regimen for previous months. Please refer to detailed instructions and demonstration photos on page 221 to begin your regimen.

Remember, you are gradually working up to the following schedule for each strength-training exercise (except push-ups):

First set:	8 to 12 repetitions Rest for one to two minutes
Second set:	8 to 12 repetitions Rest for one to two minutes
Third set:	8 to 12 repetitions Rest for one to two minutes

Strength training (Do each exercise on the days indicated)

EXERCISE	DAYS OF WEEK	6TH MONTH WEIGHTS
1. BICEPS (ARMS)	W	12 lb.
2. DELTOIDS (SHOULDERS)	W	5 lb.

3. ERECTOR SPINAE (BACK)	W	½ lb. ankle weight HANDS & KNEES POSITION
4. TRICEPS (ARM)	W	one 18 lb. body bar
5. PECS (CHEST)	W	8–10 lb.
6. ABS	M, W, F, Sa	2½ lb. ankle weight
7. PUSH-UPS	Sa	30 reps
8. SQUATS	M, F	two 10 lb. weights
9. OUTER THIGH	M, F	2½ lb. ankle weight
10. INNER THIGH	M, F	2½ lb. ankle weight

Flexibility training (Do each exercise on the days indicated)

EXERCISE	DAYS OF WEEK
1. STANDING LONG STRETCH (FULL BODY)	T, Th, Sa, Su
2. CALF STRETCH (LOWER BACK OF LEG)	T, Th, Sa, Su
3. HAMSTRING STRETCH (BACK OF THE THIGH, LOWER BACK, BUTTOCKS)	T, W, Th, Sa, Su
4. QUAD STRETCH (FRONT OF THE THIGH)	T, Th, Sa, Su
5. LONG STRETCH (FULL BODY)	M, T, Th, F, Sa, Su
6. OUTER THIGH (IT BAND)	M, T, Th, F, Sa, Su
7. BOW (BACK, GLUTEALS)	M, T, W, Th, F, Sa, Su
8. STATIC (LEGS AND BACK)	M, T, W, Th, F, Sa, Su
9. INNER THIGH	M, T, Th, F, Sa, Su
10. TRICEPS (UPPER BACK OF ARM)	M, T, W, Th, F, Sa, Su

Sixth Month

Your Exercise Program

Description of Exercises

STRENGTH TRAINING

1. Biceps (upper front of arm)
   "Bicep Curl"
- Arms down by sides, palms up.
- Knees slightly bent.
- Elbows anchored at waist.
- Curl weights to shoulders.
- Return to starting position.
- Each repetition is slow.

2. Deltoids (shoulders)
   "Lateral Raises"
- Arms at sides, knees bent.
- With elbows slightly bent, pull weights to sides at shoulder level.
- Return to starting position.
- Relax with shoulder rolls.
- You may lift front and shoulder level for the anterior deltoids.

3. Erector Spinae, gluteals (back)
   "Cross Alternate Lift"
- Lie face down on the floor.
- Slowly lift right arm and left leg. Hold for 3 seconds.
- Return to starting position.
- Lift left arm and right leg. Hold for 3 seconds.
- Return to starting position.
- To progress, add a light ankle weight or start at hands and knees, lifting alternate arm and leg.

4. Triceps (upper back of arm) "Supine Triceps Extensions"

- Lie on your back, knees bent, elbows straight up and anchored over the shoulders.
- Hold one weight with both hands.
- Slowly extend arms upward, keeping elbows slightly bent.
- Return slowly to starting position.

5. Pectorals (chest) "Pec Fly"

- Lie on your back, knees bent.
- Arms over chest and elbows. Keep elbows "soft," not locked.
- Arms slowly open out to side in line with the shoulders. Don't touch the floor.
- Pull slowly back to center over chest.

6a. Abdominal (front torso) "Ab Curl"

- Lie on back, knees bent.
- Hands behind head with elbows, out to the side. Do not pull on your head.
- Curl up to feel the torso tighten.
- Release the contraction back halfway and repeat curls.
- Arms may be extended forward for an easier curl.

6b. Abdominal (front torso) "Hip Lifts"

- Begin on hands and knees with hips down.
- Hands are under the shoulders.
- Slowly lower, leading with the chest and not the nose. Head stays up to keep your spine aligned.
- Push up to starting position.
- If this position is too challenging, try standing and pushing against the wall.

7. Anterior deltoid, biceps, triceps, trapezius, rhomboids (upper body) "Push-ups"

- Begin on hands and knees with hips down.
- Hands are under the shoulders.
- Slowly lower, leading with the chest and not the nose. Head stays up to keep your spine aligned.
- Push up to starting position.
- If this position is too challenging, try standing and pushing against the wall.

8. Quadriceps, hamstrings, gluteals (legs) "Squat"

- Stand with feet shoulder-width apart.
- Sit back, pushing buttocks back and keeping the knee over the ankle.
- Do not let the knee move forward over the toe.
- Slowly return to standing position, squeezing the buttocks. Repeat.

9. Outer thigh "Leg lifts"

- Lie on side.
- Slowly lift top leg with toe pointing down.
- Return to starting position.
- Progress by adding ankle weight for more resistance.

10. Inner thighs "Leg abduction/adduction"

- Lie on back with hands under hips to protect the back.
- Feet over chest.
- Slowly open legs and return to center. Knees are slightly flexed.

FLEXIBILITY TRAINING

1. Standing Long Stretch
(Full body)

- Stand with feet shoulder-width apart.
- Stretch up and inhale deeply.
- Lower arms and exhale.
- Repeat 3 times.

2. Calf Stretch
(Lower back of leg)

- Step 3 feet forward with front leg bent and back leg straight.
- Toes should be facing forward.
- Hold 15–20 seconds.
- Repeat both sides 2–3 times.

3. Hamstring Stretch (Back of the thigh, lower back, buttocks)

- Feet shoulder-width apart.
- Knees are slightly bent.
- Stretch up with both arms over head. Inhale.
- Slowly lower forward to let hands touch floor.
- Knees bent. Hold 3 seconds.
- Return to standing position.
- Repeat 2–3 times.

4. Quad Stretch (Front of the thigh)

- Balance on right leg with knee bent.
- Pull up left foot behind the hip and hold for 10–15 seconds.
- Knees are close to center.
- Try to balance without holding on to a chair to involve more muscles.
- Repeat on both sides 2–3 times.

5. Long Stretch
(Full body)

- Lie on your back on the floor.
- Hands overhead.
- Breathe deeply; hold and exhale.
- Reach with your arms to open the torso.

6. Outer Thigh
(IT Band)

- On your back, pull in the right knee and then pull across your body.
- Repeat 2–3 times on both sides.
- Hold.

7. Bow
(Back, gluteals)

- Face down on floor.
- Sit back on feet, head down, and stretch arms over head.
- Breathe deeply.
- Reach forward with arms.

8. Static (Legs and back)

- Sit with left leg out to side.
- Right leg may be bent.
- Stretch up to over head and inhale deeply.
- Exhale as you bend toward extended leg.
- Repeat 2–3 times, holding 15–20 seconds.

9. Inner Thigh

- Sit with soles of feet together.
- Inhale and exhale, gently leaning forward to stretch.
- Hold for 10–15 seconds.
- Repeat 2–3 times, stretching deeper each time.

10. Triceps
(upper back of arm)

- Pull right elbow straight up next to ear.
- Gently pull with the left hand.
- Hold 10–15 seconds.
- Repeat 2 times on each side.

COMPARISON OF WORLD-VIEWS

	GOD	HUMANITY	NATURE
NATURALISM:	God does not exist (atheism) Man cannot/does not know if God exists (agnosticism). The idea of God is a creation of man.	**ESSENCE:** Totally material/physical **BEHAVIOR:** Self-directed **ETHICS:** Self-determined **FUTURE:** Life ends at death	**ESSENCE:** Eternal, uncreated matter **BEHAVIOR:** All events governed by innate physical laws
TRANSCENDENTALISM:	**ESSENCE:** Impersonal force/ Spirit within all things **ATTRIBUTES:** Beyond morality and human categories **ACTIONS:** Moves all things toward unity	**ESSENCE:** Spiritual/psychic; uncreated part of divine oneness **BEHAVIOR:** Human ethics unnecessary; goal is for self-realization of divinity and unity **FUTURE:** Eternal existence; successive incarnations until enlightenment	**ESSENCE:** Physical realm either an illusion or a manifestation of divinity **BEHAVIOR:** Laws of nature limited to physical realm; not a reflection of true reality

	GOD	HUMANITY	NATURE
THEISM:	**ESSENCE:** Personal spirit, uncreated, eternal **ATTRIBUTES:** Benevolent, holy, just **ACTIONS:** Creator/sustainer of physical realm; source/standard of truth and morality	**ESSENCE:** Composite of spiritual/material; created by God and for God **BEHAVIOR:** Ethics determined by God; individual's life judged by God **FUTURE:** Eternal life with God or (some) eternal judgment	**ESSENCE:** Physical realm created by God from nothing **BEHAVIOR:** Physical realm sustained and ordered by God's character; mankind given mandate to care for created world.
BIBLICAL WORLD-VIEW: (A type of Theism)	See Theism above; also: Triune nature of God Personal spirit, uncreated, eternal **ATTRIBUTES:** Involved in the affairs of creation 1. Reveals His character/will through the Scriptures 2. Redeems humanity through the sacrifice of Christ 3. Judges all humanity 4. Benevolent, holy, just	See Theism above; also: **ESSENCE:** Created in God's image/likeness; corrupted by sin; separated from God **BEHAVIOR:** Ethics determined by God's will communicated through the Scriptures **FUTURE:** Eternal life with God for the redeemed; eternal judgment for all others	See Theism above; also: **ESSENCE:** Physical realm corrupted by man's sin **BEHAVIOR:** Physical realm to be restored to perfect state

NOTES

PART ONE:
MY FIRST STEPS ON THE PATHWAY
TOWARD HEALTH AND HEALING

1. Candace B. Pert, Ph.D., *Molecules of Emotion* (New York: Touchstone, 1999), 187–188.
2. Katharina Dalton, M.D., *Once a Month* (n.p.: Hunter House, 1998).
3. Jim Parker, "Darvon, Darvocet and Other Prescription Painkillers," Do It Now Foundation (July 2000): retrieved April 4, 2002, from www.doitnow.org/pages/157.html
4. Ibid.
5. Neal Barnard, M.D., *Food for Life: How the New Four Food Groups Can Save Your Life* (New York: Crown Trade Paperbacks, 1993).
6. Walter C. Willett, M.D., *Eat, Drink and Be Healthy* (New York: Simon & Schuster, 2001).
7. Barnard, *Food for Life: How the New Four Food Groups Can Save Your Life,* xiv.
8. "The New Four Food Groups," retrieved March 5, 2002, from www.pcrm.org/health/VSK/VSK9.html.
9. Willett, *Eat, Drink and Be Healthy,* inside front book jacket, 11.
10. *Stedmans's Medical Dictionary,* 27th Edition, 2000.
11. Dean Ornish, *Dr. Dean Ornish's Program for Reversing Heart Disease* (New York: Random House, 1990).
12. "Research Overview," Ornish Program History of Research, retrieved February 2, 2002, from www.pmri.org/story.htm.

PART TWO:
AMERICA'S HEALTH AND HEALING CRISIS

1. National Center for Health Statistics (NCHS), Vital Statistics System.
2. "The Burden of Chronic Diseases and Their Risk Factor, National and State Perspectives 2002," retrieved April 7, 2002, from www.cdc.gov/nccdphp/burdenbook2202/preface.
3. Ibid.
4. Ibid.
5. Daniel Redwood interview with Andrew Weil, M.D., 1995. Retrieved April 19, 2002, from www.drredwood.com/interviews/weil1.
6. Frijof Capra, *The Turning Point,* (New York: A Bantam Book, published by arrangement with Simon & Schuster, 1988), 136.
7. *Report of the Royal Commission on Aboriginal Peoples,* Royal Commission on Aboriginal Peoples, volume 3: Gathering Strength, 2.2 The Determinants of Health. Retrieved March 28, 2002, from www.indigenous.bc.ca. Available by mail from Canada Communications Group Publishing, Ottawa, Canada K1A 0S9 Cat. No. Z1-1991/1-1E, ISBN: O-660-16413-2.

8. More about Mattie Stepanek can be learned at www.bookmagazine.com/news/dec01news.

9. Howard S. Berliner, *"A Larger Perspective on the Flexner Report,"* International Journal of Health Services 5 (4) (1975): 576.

10. Ibid.

11. Julian Whitaker, M.D. "In My Own Words: Julian Whitaker, M.D." Retrieved from www.onehourinchloss.com/aboutdrwhitaker.htm.

12. Peter Chowka, addressing the Tenth Annual Convention of the American Association of Naturopathic Physicians—Naturopathic Medicine and the New Political Realities, "Where Do We Go From Here?" Retrieved from http://members.aol.com/pbchowka/new_realities.html.

13. The Report of the Royal Commission refers to three books in particular in their Notes that confirm this these historical facts: Thomas McKeown, *The Origins of Human Disease* (Oxford: Basil Blackwell, 1988); *The Rise of Population* (London: Edward Arnold, 1976); and *The Role of Medicine: Dream, Mirage or Nemesis?* (Princeton: Princeton University Press, 1979).

14. Berliner, "A Larger Perspective on the Flexner Report," 576, 583.

15. California Citizens for Health Freedom, 8048 Mamie Ave., Oroville, CA 95966. Retrieved August 22, 2002, from www.citizenshealth.org/goals.

16. Sue A. Blevins, "The Medical Monopoly: Protecting Consumers or Limiting Competition?" Retrieved from www.cato.org/pubs/pas/pa-246.

17. Peter Chowka at the Ninth Annual Convention of the American Association of Naturopathic Physicians (AANP), San Diego, CA, September 10, 1994: "National Healthcare Reform, The Hidden History, The Hidden Costs." Retrieved March 13, 2002, from http://members.aol.com/pbchowka/health_reform01.html.

18. Linda T. Kohn, Janet M. Corrigan, and Molla S. Donaldson, editors. *To Err Is Human: Building a Safer Health System.* Retrieved from http://books.nap.edu/books/0309068371/html/R1.html. The manuscript can be downloaded without charge from this address. The Governing Board of the National Research Council (whose members are drawn from the councils of the National Academy of Sciences, the National Academy of Engineering and the Institute of Medicine) approved the research project that is the subject of the report.

19. Barbara Starfield, "Is U.S. Health Really the Best in the World?", *Journal of the American Medical Association* (July 26, 2000): commentary.

20. *U.S. "Healthcare": #3 Killer.* Retrieved April 30, 2002, from www.ecologos.org/ushealth.htm.

21. For further discussion and rebuttal of Dr. Starfield's article see, *Deficiencies in U.S. Medical Care: Letters to the Editor* (November 1, 2000). Retrieved April 2, 2002, from http://jama.ama-assn.org/issues/v284n17/ffull/jlt1101-2.html

22. Jim Warren, "UK Policy Encourages Doctors to Use Respect," *Lexington Herald-Leader* (March 6, 1997): A1.

23. E. Ratcliffe Anderson, "AMA 2000: Shaping Medicine for a New Millennium," Remarks of the Executive Vice President 1998 Interim Meeting AMA House of Delegates (December 6, 1998): retrieved from www.ama-assn.org/meetings/public/int1998/news/2era12-6.htm.

24. "Attorney Nancy Lord, M.D. vs. the FDA." Retrieved April 21, 2002,

from www.Fija.org/lord.htm.

25. "Heart Disease and Stroke." Retrieved April 28, 2002, from www.researchamerica.org/publications/ResearchAmerica_Lasker_One-pager_HDS_Media_05.2002.

26. Wayne B. Jonas, M.D., and Jeffrey S. Levin, Ph.D., M.P.H., eds., *Essentials of Complementary and Alternative Medicine* (Baltimore, MD: Lippincott, Williams & Wilkins, 1999).

27. Ibid.

28. Mary-Margaret Chren, M.D. and Seth Landefeld, "Physicians' Behavior and Their Interactions With Drug Companies, A Controlled Study of Physicians Who Requested Additions to a Hospital Drug Formulary," *JAMA* 271 (1994): 684. "CONCLUSION:—Requests by physicians that drugs be added to a hospital formulary were strongly and specifically associated with the physicians' interactions with the companies manufacturing the drugs."

29. "Drug-company influence on medical education in USA," *Lancet* 356 (2000): 781. Retrieved January 15, 2002, from www.uems.be/lancet.htm. Conclusion: "A recent study completed by the US watchdog Public Citizen documents the relation between medical education activities, the pharmaceutical industry, and medical education services suppliers (MESS), which are private businesses that provide medical education...In summary, the data suggest that supplying medical education can, in this form, be a very lucrative exercise, whose most consistent client is the pharmaceutical industry... What is of most concern here is the fact that so much continuing medical education come through the filter of industry. To ensure the integrity, and the appearance of integrity, of the process of learning in medicine, physicians should do more to pay for CME themselves, just as many other professionals have to do."

30. Thomas Kuhn, "Paradigms Die Hard." Retrieved March 3, 2002, from http://hcs.harvard.edu/~hsr/99_hsr_webpage/hsr/winter97/kuhn. (This essay has been translated into sixteen languages, and has sold over a million copies—quite a feat for an intellectually demanding document.)

31. Robert Lombardi, *Professional Communications Textbook,* Chapter 10: Part C—Grammar, Syntax and Rhetorical Structures—Compare and Contrast Essay. Retrieved April 10, 2002, from www.kjist.ac.kr/~slic/est/e_textbook-EST-STW-Chapter 10-C.htm.

32. Ibid.

33. Fiscal Year 2002 Budget Request. Retrieved April 19, 2002 from http://nccam.hih.gov/ne/testimony/may2001.htm.

34. D. Eisenber, R. Davis, S. Ettner, et al., *JAMA* 280 (1998):1569–1575.

35. *CAM Facts* (September 9, 2000). Retrieved February 10, 2002, from www.faim.org/facts.htm.

36. Pert, *Molecules of Emotion,* 94.

37. Ibid., 95–96.

38. Robert E. Bjork, "When We Dead Awaken: Reviving Metaphor in Medical Writing," *JAC* (1983): retrieved April 5, 2002, from http://jac.gsu.edu/jac/4/Articles/12.

39. Ibid.

40. Pert, *Molecules of Emotion,* 187–188.

41. Capra, *The Turning Point,* 162.

42. "The Jack LaLanne Story." Retrieved April 15, 2002, from www.jacklalanne.com/biograph.html.
43. Ibid.
44. Kenneth H. Cooper, M.D., *Regaining the Power of Youth* (Nashville, TN: Thomas Nelson, Inc., 1998), 267–268.
45. Cooper Wellness. Retrieved April 4, 2001, from www.cooperwellness.com/bios.
46. Capra, *The Turning Point,* 162.

PART THREE: HOW WE HEAL

1. History of Naturopathy, retrieved April 4, 2002, from www.naturopathic.org/education/licensing/slideshow/History2.html.
2. W. C. Willett, F. Sacks, A. Trichopoulou, G. Drescher, A. Ferro-Luzzi, E. Helsing, D. Trichopoulos, "Mediterranean Diet Pyramid: A Cultural Model for Healthy Eating," *American Journal of Clinical Nutrition* 61, no. 6 suppl (1995): 1402S.
3. J. Chen, T. C. Campbell, J. Li, R. Peto, *Diet, Lifestyle, and Mortality in China, A Study of the Characteristics of 65 Chinese Counties* (Oxford, UK: Oxford University Press; Ithaca, NY: Cornell University Press; Beijing, Peoples Republic of China: Peoples Medical Publishing House, 1990).
4. Source retrieved from www.health.harvard.edu/tools/pyramid.cfm.
5. "About Chronic Disease," retrieved March 2, 2002, from www.cdc.gov/nccdphp/about.htm.
6. A Public Health Epidemic, retrieved from www.cdc.gov/nccdphp/dnpa/obesity/epidemic.htm.
7. Ibid.
8. "NIH Should Apply Its Own Criteria for Funding Research," retrieved April 20, 2002, from www.diabetes.org/meir/community/advocacy/nihcriteria.jsp.
9. Berliner, "A Larger Perspective on the Flexner Report," 573–592.
10. Retrieved from www.drbralyallergyrelief.com/info.html.
11. Ibid.
12. Melissa Diane Smith, "Against the Grain: Could Gluten Sensitivity Be Compromising Your Health?" retrieved from www.healthwell.com/delicious-online/d_backs/apr_01/nutrition.cfm.
13. Christine Gorman, "Against the Grain," *Time* (February 26, 2001): retrieved from www.time.com/time/magazine.
14. Smith, "Against the Grain: Could Gluten Sensitivity Be Compromising Your Health?"
15. National Diabetes Statistics, retrieved on April 6, 2002, from www.niddk.nih.gov/health/diabetes/pubs/dmstats/dmstats.htm.
16. Barbara Darling, "M.D.s turn to alternatives in area holistic clinics," *Nexus, Colorado's Holistic Journal* (July /August 1998): Retrieved from www.nexuspub.com/articles/1998/july98/clinic.htm.
17. Ibid.
18. Ron Rosedale, "Insulin and Its Metabolic Effects," retrieved from www.dfhi.com/interviews/rosedale.htm.

19. Khem M. Shahani, Ph.D., "Facts and Fallacies About Probiotics," a position paper distributed privately by Khem M. Shahani, Ph.D., Professor of Food Science and Technology, University of Nebraska.
20. Khem M. Shahani, Ph.D., "Nutritional, Therapeutic and Immunomodulatory Role of Probiotics (Particularly about L. acidophilus DDS-1)," paper presented at the fall convention of the American College for the Advancement in Medicine, Anaheim, CA (1997): 9.
21. "Diabetes: Health and Research Guide," *Ability Magazine* 98, no. 4 (1998).
22. Physicians Committee for Responsible Medicine, "Diet and Diabetes" (Washington, DC).
23. Herman Adlercreutz et al., "Dietary Phytoestrogens and Cancer: In Vitro and in Vivo Studies," *Journal of Steroid Biochemistry and Molecular Biology* 41, no. 3–8 (1992): 331–337; Herman Adlercreutz et al., "Urinary Excretion of Lignans and Isoflavonoid Phytoestrogens in Japanese Men and Women Consuming a Traditional Japanese Diet," *American Journal of Clinical Nutrition* 54 (1991): 1093–1100.
24. Walter Willett, M.D., "Diet and Cardiovascular Diseases (CVD)," retrieved from www.orst.edu/dept/lpi/conference/willett1.html.
25. Adlercreutz et al., "Urinary Excretion," 1093.
26. H. K. Ziel, and W. D. Finkle, "Increased Risk of Endometrial Carcinoma among Users of Conjugated Estrogens," *New England Journal of Medicine* 293, no. 23 (1975): 1167–1170.
27. Marcus Laux, N.D. and Christine Conrad, *Natural Woman, Natural Menopause* (New York: HarperCollins Publishers, 1997), 46.
28. Elizabeth Lee Vliet, M.D., *Screaming to Be Heard: Hormonal Connections Women Suspect...and Doctors Ignore* (New York: M. Evans and Company, 1995), 107.
29. John R. Lee, M.D., *Natural Progesterone: The Multiple Roles of a Remarkable Hormone,* revised ed. (Sebastopol, CA: BLL Publishing, 1993, 1997), 88.
30. Jerilynn C. Prior, M.D., "One Voice on Menopause," *JAMA* 49, no. 1 (1994): 28.
31. Ibid., 27
32. Ibid.
41. John R. Lee, M.D. with David T. Zava, Ph.D. *The Secrets of Natural Hormone Therapy: Keys to Preventing Women's Most Serious Health Problems* (Harry DeLigter Productions, 1996), two audiocassettes.
34. John R. Lee, M.D. with Virginia Hopkins, *What Your Doctor May Not Tell You About Menopause: The Breakthrough Book on Natural Progesterone.* (New York: Warner Books, 1996), 187.
35. Lee, *What Your Doctor May Not Tell You About Menopause,* 40, 42
36. Janet Raloff, "The Gender Benders, Are environmental 'hormones' emasculating wildlife?" *Science News* (January 8, 1944): Retrieved from www.sciencenews.org/sn_edpik/ls_7.htm.
37. Samuel S. Epstein, "None of Us Should Eat Extra Estrogen," *Los Angeles Times* (March 24, 1977): 5.
38. Lee, *The Secrets of Natural Hormone Therapy.*
39. Ibid.

233

40. Neal Barnard, "Using Foods Against Menstrual Pain." retrieved April 8, 2002, from www.pcrm.org/news/health000131_ftfp_ch.html.
41. Lee, *Natural Progesterone*, 25.
42. Lee, *The Secrets of Natural Hormone Therapy*.
43. Ibid.
44. Lee, *Natural Progesterone*, 25.
45. Pert, *Molecules of Emotion*, 188–189.
46. Robert D. Orr, M.D, "Personal and Professional Integrity in Clinical Medicine," Jack W. Provonsha Lectureship, School of Medicine, Loma Linda University, Alumni Postgraduate Convention 1992. Retrieved March 19, 2002 from www.llu.edu/llu/bioethics/prov2_92.htm.
47. Pert, *Molecules of Emotion*, 187.
48. Ibid.
49. "Harriet Tubman (c. 1820–1913)," retrieved September 6, 2002, from http://faculty.brenan.edu/lewis/tubman.html.
50. Ibid.
51. "How It Began," retrieved March 2, 2002, from www.vimclinic.org/james.htm.
52. James A. Blumenthal et al., "Depression and Vascular Function in Older Adults," *NCMJ* (March/April 2001): 95–98. Retrieved online February 2, 2002, from www.ncmedicaljournal.com/mar-apr-01/ar080301.pdf.
53. Pert, *Molecules of Emotion*, 64.
54. Ibid.
55. "Exercise Boosts Brain Power," retrieved January 15, 2002, from http://news.bbc.co.uk/hi/english/sci/tech/newsid_406000/406334.stm.
56. Ibid.

PART FOUR: A 180-DAY JOURNEY

1. Adapted from Harold L. Willmington, *Willmington's Complete Guide to Bible Knowledge* (Wheaton, IL: Tyndale House Publishers, Inc., 1991), 265–267.
2. Ibid., 277–280.
3. Sereana Howard Dresback and Amy Rossi, "Phytochemicals—Vitamins of the Future?", Ohio State University Extension Fact Sheet, retrieved online on September 5, 2002, from http://ohioline.osu.edu/hyg-fact/5000/5050.html.

APPENDIX: COMPARISON OF WORLD-VIEWS

1. W. Gary Phillips, Th.D. and William E. Brown, Ph.D., *Making Sense of Your World: A Biblical Worldview* (Salem, WI: Sheffield Publishing Company, 1996), 94–95.

Ministry
Information

FOR ARTICLES ON HEALTH AND HEALING, and for more information on Dr. Terry Dorian and Health Begins in Him Ministries, go to http://www.healthbeginsinhim.org.

For information and recommendations concerning integrative physicians and nonphysician health practitioners, health and healing services, nutritional supplements, whole foods, supplies for food preparation and products that enhance natural living go to http://www.terrydorian.com.

For an extensive bibliography of valuable related materials the author has compiled concerning specific health issues, please access her website as well.

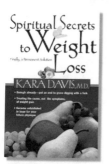

Your Walk With God Can Be Even Deeper...

With *Charisma* magazine, you'll be informed and inspired by the features and stories about what the Holy Spirit is doing in the lives of believers today.

Each issue:

- Brings you exclusive world-wide reports to rejoice over.
- Keeps you informed on the latest news from a Christian perspective.
- Includes miracle-filled testimonies to build your faith.
- Gives you access to relevant teaching and exhortation from the most respected Christian leaders of our day.

Call 1-800-829-3346 for 3 FREE trial issues
Offer #A2CCHB

If you like what you see, then pay the invoice of $22.97 (**saving over 51% off the cover price**) and receive 9 more issues (12 in all). Otherwise, write "cancel" on the invoice, return it, and owe nothing.

Experience the Power of Spirit-Led Living

Charisma Offer #A2CCHB
P.O. Box 420234
Palm Coast, Florida 32142-0234
www.charismamag.com

1884A